THE WORLD'S CLASSICS

THE *MEDITATIONS*
OF MARCUS AURELIUS
ANTONINUS

R. B. RUTHERFORD is Tutor in Greek and Latin Literature at Christ Church, Oxford. His research interests include Homer, fifth-century Greek prose and poetry, and Plato. He is the author of *The Meditations of Marcus Aurelius: A Study*, also published by Oxford University Press (1989).

OXFORD WORLD'S CLASSICS

*For over 100 years Oxford World's Classics have brought
readers closer to the world's great literature. Now with over 700
titles—from the 4,000-year-old myths of Mesopotamia to the
twentieth century's greatest novels—the series makes available
lesser-known as well as celebrated writing.*

*The pocket-sized hardbacks of the early years contained
introductions by Virginia Woolf, T. S. Eliot, Graham Greene,
and other literary figures which enriched the experience of reading.
Today the series is recognized for its fine scholarship and
reliability in texts that span world literature, drama and poetry,
religion, philosophy and politics. Each edition includes perceptive
commentary and essential background information to meet the
changing needs of readers.*

OXFORD WORLD'S CLASSICS

The Meditations *of* Marcus Aurelius Antoninus

Translated by the late
A. S. L. FARQUHARSON

AND A

Selection from the Letters of Marcus and Fronto

Translated by R. B. RUTHERFORD

With Introduction and Notes by
R. B. RUTHERFORD

OXFORD
UNIVERSITY PRESS

OXFORD
UNIVERSITY PRESS

Great Clarendon Street, Oxford OX2 6DP

Oxford University Press is a department of the University of Oxford.
It furthers the University's objective of excellence in research, scholarship,
and education by publishing worldwide in

Oxford New York

Athens Auckland Bangkok Bogotá Buenos Aires Calcutta
Cape Town Chennai Dar es Salaam Delhi Florence Hong Kong Istanbul
Karachi Kuala Lumpur Madrid Melbourne Mexico City Mumbai
Nairobi Paris São Paulo Singapore Taipei Tokyo Toronto Warsaw

with associated companies in Berlin Ibadan

Oxford is a registered trade mark of Oxford University Press
in the UK and in certain other countries

Published in the United States
by Oxford University Press Inc., New York

Translation of the *Meditations* of Marcus Aurelius Antoninus
by the late A. S. L. Farquharson © Oxford University Press 1944
Translation of a selection from the Correspondence of Marcus
Cornelius Fronto and Marcus Aurelius Antoninus © R. B. Rutherford 1989
Introduction and notes © R. B. Rutherford 1989

British Library Cataloguing in Publication Data

Data available

Library of Congress Cataloging in Publication Data

Data available

ISBN 0-19-283907-1

7 9 10 8 6

Printed in Great Britain by
Clays Ltd, St Ives plc

PREFACE

In 1906 the World's Classics series issued a translation of the *Meditations* or 'Thoughts' of the emperor Marcus Aurelius by John Jackson; in 1944 Oxford University Press published a large and beautifully produced commentary on the work by A. S. L. Farquharson, which included a new text and translation. Both works have, however, been out of print for many years. That Marcus Aurelius' little book deserves a place in the new World's Classics series would hardly be denied; in the introduction to this volume I try to explain what interest and value the work has for the modern reader. The choice of Farquharson's translation in preference to Jackson's or another's is a natural one; not only is it more recent and more readable, but it rests on a lifetime's labour to understand and elucidate this difficult text. Although both Roman imperial history and literary scholarship have come a long way since Farquharson, any student of the *Meditations* must still gratefully consult his commentary, and it is a pleasure to be able to use his version as the basis of this work, which will, I hope, help others to see why Farquharson cared so much for this author, on whom he worked more or less continuously for much of his scholarly life.

Bt. Lt.-Col. Arthur Spenser Loat Farquharson was born in 1871, and educated at Portsmouth Grammar School, Rochester King's School, and University College, Oxford, where he took a double first in Classical Honour Mods and Literae Humaniores, graduating in 1894. After a short period as Assistant Master at Trinity College, Glenalmond, he returned to Oxford and served for many years at his old college as Lecturer in Classics and later in Philosophy. He also served in the Territorial Army (rising to Major by 1914 and Brevet Lieutenant-Colonel in 1918); he was twice mentioned in dispatches, received the CBE in 1919, and was an Officer of the Légion d'Honneur. He was attached to the War Office (GSO 2 and GSO 1) from 1915 to 1921.

Besides his work on the Stoic emperor, he published a scholarly
edition of Aristotle's treatise on the motions of animals which has
only recently been superseded. He died in 1942; his commentary
and a short biographical account of Marcus Aurelius were seen
through the Press by friends. It seems clear that, himself both a
soldier and a scholar, he felt a special affinity with the emperor,
whose philosophic concerns were disrupted by military
obligations.

The translation remains unaltered, though I have occasionally
offered corrections or expressed doubts about a rendering. The
introduction and notes are entirely my responsibility; they are
mainly intended to help the newcomer to see what Marcus is doing and to grasp the point of certain names and allusions. I have
been reasonably generous, as far as the scope of the series allows,
in providing cross-references to other ancient authors and occasionally to modern books; but of course this does not amount to
a proper commentary.

This volume also contains a limited selection (less than 10 per
cent of the whole) from the letters of Fronto, Marcus' tutor and
lifelong friend. These I have translated myself. The correspondence also contains many replies from Marcus, some of
which are included; although they are mostly of an earlier date
than the *Meditations*, they provide a precious insight to the other
side of his character and also have considerable literary and social
interest. These letters were discovered in a number of unexamined
manuscripts at the beginning of the nineteenth century, and have
still not received the full-scale linguistic and historical commentary they need—facts which may surprise those who assume that
classical studies can offer nothing new for modern researchers to
find out or write about.

I am grateful to a number of friends and colleagues who have
looked at and offered suggestions on parts of the work, and to
Hilary Feldman of Oxford University Press, for suggesting the
idea in the first place.

R.B.R.

CONTENTS

To the one of concern:

This book is the crystallization of the wisdom of the most renown sceptor of the ancient Roman Empire.

Hope you may find daily comfort and drink from the spring of intelligence to complete the arduous course of the pursuit of excellency and happiness.

Love,

Shm

INTRODUCTION

'What but the consciousness of duty could induce the aged philosopher to march hour after hour among the forests and swamps of the almost uncivilized Danubian lands?' These admiring words from the greatest ancient historian of the past century[1] capture at least some of the fascination of Marcus Aurelius' career for the modern student. Here if ever in the early empire we meet a philosopher on the throne; a man who took the task of ruling seriously, who tirelessly sacrificed his own comfort and leisure to administration and, for many years of his reign, to unproductive and exhausting defensive campaigns.

The work we call the *Meditations* of Marcus Aurelius was composed at least partly during the German campaigns, which dominated the last years of Marcus' life. Since he more than once refers to his 'old age' in these pages, and since he was only 59 when he died, it is probably safe to assign the work to his last decade, the 170s AD. But the reader who opens this book with the expectation of finding out what Marcus thought about Roman methods of warfare, about German battlefields, about imperial defence strategy or the structure of the high command, will be disappointed on all counts. The *Meditations* are both more and less revealing than, for instance, the self-exonerating account Julius Caesar wrote of his Gallic campaigns, or the journals of a modern general or statesman writing with an eye on posterity. More revealing, because Marcus was writing for himself, and seems to have had no thought of making his reflections available to a wider audience in his own lifetime or thereafter. Less revealing, because for the most part he rigidly excludes the details of contemporary events, the incidents of politics and warfare, things which must have been in his mind but which were not appropriate to the pages of his philosophic

[1] M. Rostovtzeff, *Social and Economic History of the Roman Empire*, 2nd edn. (Oxford, 1957), 108.

journal. A modern reader will want to know, then, what kind of work this is, and what can in fact be learned or deduced from it about the author's beliefs and experiences.

The title *Meditations* is not of ancient origin. Quite probably the work had no title in the author's own mind, any more than it had a fixed shape, length, or plan. We may reasonably guess that it was a sort of cross between a diary and a commonplace-book. At the end of the day, the emperor would record a few reflections and admonish himself to observe certain precepts and ethical rules which he might have neglected in the course of the day. We know that this practice was common among philosophically trained, well-educated men of the early Roman empire: it is in fact recommended by the Stoic teacher Epictetus, whose works were familiar to Marcus.[2] At times the emperor would copy out a few quotations, in poetry or prose, usually of moral import (esp. vii. 38–42, xi. 30–2, 34, 36–9). At other times he would formulate his own versions, often laconic or epigrammatic, of philosophic sentiments. Only occasionally does his writing become more expansive, his style more ambitious; perhaps only occasionally did he have time and enthusiasm enough to develop a topic at greater length, and try his hand at a piece of sustained argument or exposition. For the most part, his thoughts are brief and fragmentary, as though he wrote only three or four lines at a time.

In our modern editions, and in this translation, the work is divided into twelve 'books', and each book into numbered 'chapters'. But this is a purely modern device, intended to make clear to the reader where one reflection ends and another begins. Nor does 'chapter' seem quite the right word for what may in some cases be an epigram only six words long. Comparison with Pascal's *Pensées* or La Rochefoucauld's *Maximes* may give a clearer picture of how the work may be read, though both analogies are imprecise. At any rate, it is unlikely that Marcus thought of himself as writing in books and chapters (the obscure

---

[2] Compare Horace, *Satires* I. iv. 133–9, Seneca, *On anger* iii. 36, Epictetus II. xviii. 12 ff., III. v. 11, IV. iv. 7, IV. vi. 32.

headings which precede books ii and iii in the manuscripts may only indicate use of a new roll or change of location); but the division is traditional and makes precise reference to a particular 'thought' more straightforward. What does need emphasis, however, is that the individual books (apart from book i, of which more below) have no unity or specific theme; we are not dealing with a work such as Lucretius' *On the Nature of the Universe* or Pliny's *Natural History*, ordered treatises in which a particular topic is discussed in a particular book. The arrangement of the *Meditations* seems almost entirely random: it may follow the order of composition, but this is impossible to prove and probably does not matter very much. On the other hand, Marcus does tend to return again and again to certain favourite themes, and cross-reference from one passage to another can help us understand his views on a given point more clearly. In the notes to this translation I have tried to give some help in this process of cross-reference.

Marcus was a Roman emperor, and readers are often surprised to learn that he wrote the *Meditations* entirely in Greek. Surely at the end of a long day the effort of translating his thoughts into a foreign tongue must have been thoroughly unwelcome? In fact there are a number of factors which make this choice of language less freakish than it seems at first sight. For one thing, Roman intellectuals were educated from an early age in Greek, and often acquired considerable fluency. Cicero peppers his private letters with Greek phrases, and Marcus and Fronto exchange Greek dialogues and letters in the emperor's youth. The older, richer Greek tongue had something of the sophisticated *cachet* at Rome that French possessed in the European capitals during the eighteenth century. Secondly, a ruler and overseer of diplomatic business in the Empire such as Marcus would be constantly dealing with Greek speakers—ambassadors, orators, grandees visiting the imperial court. Greek, far more than Latin, was the *lingua franca*, the *koine* or 'common tongue', of the Mediterranean. Thirdly and most important, Marcus was writing about philosophic subjects, and Greek was the language of philosophy. Stoicism, the doctrines of which permeate the *Meditations*, was a Greek school of thought, and most of the philosophers worth reading had written in Greek, including the Stoic Epictetus. Although important work had been done, above all by Cicero, towards the creation of a Latin philosophic vocabulary, many of the technical terms still could not be rendered into Latin with any degree of ease or naturalness.[3] Even Roman philosophic writers often wrote in Greek: a distinguished example is Brutus, the assassin of Julius Caesar. Marcus' choice, therefore, is not so surprising, and although his style may sometimes seem awkward and inelegant, it is certainly not incoherent or ungrammatical.

We may next consider the principles of Stoicism, which so pre-occupied Marcus. Only a brief and highly simplified account can be given here.[4] For the Stoics, man was above all else a reasoning animal, and this rationality was the divine spark that elevated him above the beasts. Reason could and should control and discipline the unruly passions; to 'live according to nature', a regular formulation of the Stoic ideal, meant for them not self-indulgence or bestiality, but life according to *reason*. Reason taught man to live a life of virtue, to behave justly, sociably, unselfishly, truthfully. Virtue was its own reward, and was unaffected by external conditions; the virtuous and wise man would be happy and self-sufficient, even if mocked, humiliated, and mistreated by the deluded and ignorant mob. External 'goods' such as wealth, reputation, high office, and even good health, though highly valued by popular opinion, were of no moral value (but the Stoics admitted that they were preferable to their opposites). Stoicism was a stern philosophy, normally allowing no place to ideas such as rewards for the virtuous in the after-life. Most Stoics held that the soul survived the dissolution of the body, but was then resolved into the elements of its being and reunited with the substance of the universe—immortality of

[3] For a very full and helpful account of these questions see Jorma Kaimio, *The Romans and the Greek Language* (Helsinki, 1979). The Prefaces to Cicero's philosophic works are revealing documents, though tinged with a self-defensive attitude to Latin. Lucretius complains of the *patrii sermonis egestas* ('the poverty of our native tongue'), *On the Nature of the Universe*, i. 832.

[4] Works cited in the Bibliography by Sandbach, Long, and Long and Sedley give fuller details on the doctrines and adherents of Stoicism.

a kind, but with little or no place for personal awareness of continuing existence. As for theology, the Stoics would at once agree that the universe was divine and controlled by divine providence; but they saw this providence not as a benign and watchful deity observing his creation with just or merciful concern, but as a much more impersonal and mechanistic process. God was not transcendent, outside his creation, but immanent in it: Stoicism was ruthlessly materialist. Even the Universe would finally be dissolved in a great conflagration, after which it would eventually be renewed—according to some, taking exactly the form it had had before, with the world and everything in it following exactly the same motions.

With external goods, even others' good opinion, dismissed from consideration, and with no hope of an immortal afterlife, overwhelming importance must be attached to the individual's moral choice. All Stoic writers dwell with special emphasis on the need to train one's responses, so as to respond willingly and correctly, spurning easier but more degenerate impulses. Not everybody could achieve the goal of wisdom, and become a *sapiens* or 'wise man' (an ideal state which many doubted whether anyone in history had ever reached!), but from the second century BC onwards, much attention was paid to the needs of the *proficiens*, the man who is 'making progress' towards virtue. That progress would be a perpetual struggle, a battle within the soul. 'Life is a kind of military service', as the Stoic Seneca put it (*Letters*, xcvi. 5), a war against the rebellious passions and also a defensive campaign to repel external distractions and temptations. In Seneca's letters to the aspiring philosopher Lucilius, we see one Stoic helping another to fight his way towards a virtuous way of life. In Marcus' *Meditations*, the author is reproving, exhorting, criticizing *himself*: he is disturbed if he has fallen short, he warns himself to prepare for the challenges which the next day may bring, and he sets his own trivial activities or concerns in the vaster context of the passing of generations, even the decay and disintegration of the world itself. In his nightly journal the Stoic emperor strives to break free from more petty, everyday anxieties and to turn his mind to eternity.

If this reading of the *Meditations* is correct, then there is no question of the work setting out a systematic body of doctrine, or even a looser series of principles and precepts (such as we find in Epictetus' *Handbook* or *Manual*). The purpose of Marcus' book is much more therapeutic. The author repeatedly returns to certain topics of particular relevance to his own moral difficulties, but he is not trying to preach to all men. In some passages he makes explicit the moral defect which he needs to combat. In iv. 49 he writes: 'in every event which leads you to sorrow, remember to use this principle . . .'; in x. 34 a quotation from the *Iliad* 'is reminder enough to dispel sorrow and fear'; in xi. 18 he sets out ten prescriptions against anger, which was a central topic in ancient moralistic writing. The soul, he writes elsewhere, is 'dyed' to match the character of its inner thoughts: 'dye it, then, in a succession of imaginations like these . . .' (v. 16); and similarly in iii. 4 he longs to be 'dyed with justice to the core'.

A particularly suggestive passage is iii. 13. 'As doctors have their instruments and scalpels always at hand to meet sudden demands for treatment, so do you have your doctrines ready in order to recognize the divine and human, and so to do everything . . . mindful of the bond which unites the divine and human.' The medical analogy for philosophy, the art which can heal and cure the sicknesses of the soul, is traditional, but this and other passages make clear that Marcus sees his writing as self-therapy. So also in v. 9: 'don't return to Philosophy as to a schoolmaster, but as a man with sore eyes to the sponge and salve, as another to a poultice, another to a fomentation'. The simple and fundamental truths which philosophy provides 'will suffice at once by their presence to wash away all sorrow, and to send you back without repugnance to the life to which you return' (iv. 3).

What topics, then, may the reader expect to find as he or she reads the *Meditations*? Apart from the occasional rash of quotations, there are passages in which the author urges himself to do his duty and to perform social and unselfish acts; passages in which he bitterly rebukes himself for failure to do so, or for paying too much attention to what other people expect or think of him; and passages in which he sourly comments on the behaviour of others, who fall short of philosophic virtue—though he never identifies or criticizes them individually. There is contemplation of the physical workings of the universe, reflection on the transience of human life, meditation on the prospect of death. There are also some more intriguing passages in which he alludes to his own rank, to the life of the court, and to the relation between philosophy and power. Thus from viii. 9 ('let no one any longer hear you finding fault with your life in a palace; nay, do not even hear yourself') we may reasonably deduce that the emperor was not always wholly content with his imperial role; and chapters such as ix. 29, x. 27, and x. 36 suggest impatience with some of the flattery and hypocrisy that inevitably surrounded even a good emperor. In xi. 7 he writes that 'no other calling in life is so fitted for the practice of philosophy as this in which you now find yourself'—a view strikingly at variance with that held by many Romans, who felt that philosophy with its idealism and impractical speculations actually unfitted a man for the realities of public life. But elsewhere he seems to take a more pessimistic view himself: his calling may conflict with his philosophic pursuits (vi. 12, viii. 1); he has no time to read and study as he would wish (iii. 3, iii. 14, viii. 8); he refers to regular longings for withdrawal to a country retreat (iv. 3); in his gloomier moods he can question whether even a good man and a philosopher can change men's opinions (ix. 29). There is, of course, no need to reconcile these conflicting attitudes: we can expect the *Meditations*, probably compiled over a period of some years, to reflect the author's shifting moods. But since Marcus never gives the date and circumstances of an entry, it is fruitless to attempt to relate these moods to the changing course of a campaign or to specific political events.

The reader seeking biographical details can derive more information from book i, which has a rather different character from the rest of the collection. Although also composed in Greek and clearly by the same author, it has a more coherent shape and may well have been planned as a unity. Here the emperor goes through a list of his closer relatives and a number of his teachers, recording what he owes to each—in some cases a specific lesson, the loan of a book or an aspect of his upbringing, but more often

a general moral example. The book is arranged in approximately
chronological order (grandfather, father, mother, etc.) and
culminates in the two longest and most important entries, in
which Marcus recounts what he owes to Antoninus Pius (his
predecessor as emperor) and to the gods (i. 16 and 17). But even
in these longer chapters there is no rational order to what he
records: he seems to be writing things down almost as they come
into his head, and some references are completely opaque to us
(e.g. in i. 16 'the way he treated the tax-collector who apologized
at Tusculum . . .'). But the first book as a whole, just because
it is so private and intimate a document, gives us unique access
to the mind of an ancient ruler, and there is much to be learned
from it about Marcus' attitude and principles. There are even
some tantalizing details about his sexual life and his religious
experiences: the latter were obviously of importance to him,
though the references are frustratingly obscure.

In vi. 48, Marcus seems to set out the programme for book i.
'Whenever you desire to cheer yourself [he writes there], think
upon the merits of those who are alive with you: the energy of
one, for instance, the modesty of another . . . For nothing is so
cheering as the images of the virtues shining in the character of
contemporaries and meeting so far as possible in a group.
Therefore you should keep them ready to your hand.' This
chapter clearly shows what value the catalogue that we call book
i must have had for Marcus, and it is probably no accident that
a nearby chapter (vi. 30) looks like a preliminary draft of the
fuller portrait of Antoninus Pius in i. 16. Book i, therefore, was
probably conceived as a whole, and composed independently of
the emperor's regular commonplace-book, though preserved
with the rest.

It will by now be clear that there are some questions we might
like to ask to which the *Meditations* will not give us the answer.
We will not learn from this work what Marcus thought of the
revolt of Avidius Cassius, or why he chose his son, the deplorable
Commodus, to be his successor. Nor can we learn anything about
his day-to-day conduct of the task of ruling, though we can
obviously deduce a certain amount from the scrupulousness and

the sense of duty which we can discern throughout his work. Some things we might expect to find are surprisingly absent: no references to the doubts cast on his wife Faustina's fidelity (perhaps because he took it for granted); and only one rather vague allusion to the Christians (perhaps because at this date they did not seem very important). There is a strong tendency to cut out everyday events and trivial incidents: though in- dividual reflections were no doubt often prompted by a specific encounter or some upsetting development, Marcus does not think it necessary to dwell on the events of the day, and outside book i we cannot trace his views on particular contemporaries. He preferred to purge his mind of the day's vexations, to take refuge in more general and more absolute concerns. 'You have the power,' he told himself, 'to strip off many superfluities which trouble you and are wholly in your own judgement; and you will make a large room at once for yourself by embracing in your thought the whole Universe, grasping ever-continuing Time and pondering the rapid change in the parts of each object, how brief the interval from birth to dissolution, and the time before birth a yawning gulf even as the period after dissolution equally boundless' (ix. 32). The trivia of everyday existence are set in a majestic though melancholy perspective.

But if we cannot use the *Meditations* to fill the many gaps in our narrative of Marcus' reign and campaigns, that does not mean that the work's historical value is negligible. In general terms, if not in particular, we can see what kind of monarch Marcus wished to be, for he paints a full and vivid picture of Antoninus Pius, and tells himself to be in all things his pupil. He thanks the gods 'that though I was often angry with Rusticus I never went to extremes for which I should have been sorry' (i. 17), and he frequently insists on the need for self-restraint and patience in dealing with his associates (iv. 28, vii. 62, etc.); from his own words we can deduce that he often found it hard to restrain his temper, and hence that the many references to anger in the *Meditations* are not merely conventional. Again, he quite frequently mentions the emperors who ruled before himself, and although some of his verdicts are unsurprising (as when he condemns Nero in iii. 16), it is striking that he never refers to the more virtuous emperors as divine (see iv. 32; 33; viii. 5, 'in a little while you will be no one and nowhere, even as Hadrian and Augustus are no more'). In his own lifetime Marcus paid little regard to the imperial cult, and through the *Meditations* we can see that this reflected his own sombre convictions: Trajan, Hadrian, Antoninus all died at the appointed time, and so will he.

More broadly, the *Meditations* show more clearly than almost any ancient text how important a role philosophy might play in the life of an educated man. Marcus turns naturally to Stoicism as a way of imposing meaning on the chaos of his daily concerns, as a solid structure of truths which provide some stability and consolation in a troubled life. Human beings have been placed in this world with certain duties and obligations; philosophy makes these explicit and excludes the possibility of complaint or resentment. To understand the workings of divine law, or the physical processes of Universal nature, is to become reconciled to one's own place in the ordered structure of human society and the larger order of the cosmos. Ancient thinkers would have felt no sense that some of these questions were more the province of religion than of philosophy: questions of religion and of the relation of man to god had been part of philosophic enquiry from the beginning. The intellectual classes of the Roman republic and early empire had long been conscious of what the Greek schools had to offer, and for many of them philosophy was an important part of their personal and moral lives, a source of inspiration and comfort, and a means of articulating their moral dilemmas. Although not all Romans would have accepted this further point, the Stoics insisted that philosophy was in the full sense a way of life, not something to be treated as a hobby or a purely academic discipline. Marcus agreed: 'put an end once and for all to discussion of what a good man ought to be, and *be* one' (x. 16).

So far we have considered the nature and purpose of the *Meditations*, and some of the historical and biographical interest that the work possesses. In conclusion, something needs to be said about the work's *literary* status, about the qualities which make it a classic. Many readers have been intrigued by Marcus' book for reasons related to the points made above: it brings us closer to an unusual figure, a ruler of the Roman empire, and it shows something of the difficulty of combining philosophy and supreme power. These are good and legitimate reasons for reading the *Meditations*, but they do not exhaust their appeal. The fascination of the work lies above all in the language and thought of the author. Marcus' *pensées* are varied and uneven in scale and quality: at one time he may write ten-word aphorisms and biting reflections on human weakness; at another, more extended, elegiac passages on mortality and the limits of human achievement. Vivid epigram and severe eloquence may be juxta-posed within a few pages. The imagery and metaphorical language in which Marcus describes the passage of time or the workings of nature can take the reader aback—on one page we meet wonder and delight at nature's inventiveness or her generosity (iii. 2, x. 26), on another revulsion from the sordid vileness of the material world (iv. 32, viii. 24, ix. 14). Though he is not usually the originator of the images he employs, he often gives them classic expression: the world as a stage (xii. 36, with n.), the virtuous soul as a spring of pure water (viii. 51), the anti-social man as a branch severed from a tree (xi. 8, cf. viii. 34). And some conceptions seem particularly his own: other authors in antiquity wrote of the vastness of the universe, but none expresses so regularly and with such power the claustrophobic sense of man's life as a tiny pinpoint in time, planted on a minute dot in an infinite universe prolonged through eternity (vi. 36, vii. 48-9, viii. 21, etc.).

The essentially pessimistic tone of the *Meditations* makes the work congenial to many contemplative or reflective spirits: it shares something of the gloomy eloquence of that bleakest of all religious texts, the book of Ecclesiastes. But Marcus' writing, while often despondent, is almost never despairing: man has a purpose in the Universe, and he is equipped to fulfil that pur-pose, if he only has the will to do so. Indeed, in his more positive moods, the language of Marcus' religious devotion and self-surrender seems warmer and more passionate than Stoic metaphysics might seem to justify (esp. iv. 23, v. 4).[5] Above all, however, it is the author's fierce moral commitment that can still seem admirable and impressive even to a reader who does not care about Stoic doctrine and may even be repelled by it. 'Suppose the gods take counsel about none of our concerns, I am able to take counsel about myself' (vi. 44). If we accept, however tentatively and unfashionably, that literature can be relevant to life and that readers can learn from and be inspired by the writings of the past, then Marcus Aurelius, whose clear insight into human failings, not least his own, led him not to cynical inertia but to increased resolve, may still have something to teach us today.

[5] Though for the religious note in traditional Stoicism see especially Cleanthes' *Hymn to Zeus* (*Stoicorum Veterum Fragmenta*, ed. H. von Arnim (Stuttgart, 1903–24) i. 527), especially lines 32 ff. It is translated in *The Oxford Book of Greek Verse in Translation*, ed. T. F. Higham and C. M. Bowra (Oxford, 1938), 533–7, and in part in Long and Sedley, *The Hellenistic philosophers*, i (Cambridge, 1987), 326–7.

BIOGRAPHICAL NOTE

Marcus Aurelius, born at Rome in AD 121 as Marcus Annius Verus, was of Spanish extraction, son of an ex-consul who was also brother-in-law of Antoninus Pius. He lost his father in early childhood (cf. *Meditations*, i. 2), but was soon favoured with the patronage of the emperor Hadrian, who had assumed the throne in 117. Hadrian gave him the nickname Verissimus ('most truthful' or 'most sincere of men'), and in 136 betrothed him to the daughter of L. Ceionius Commodus, consul of that year, Hadrian's proposed successor. Ceionius died in 138, whereupon Hadrian turned to the sober and trustworthy Antoninus Pius, adopting him and requiring him to adopt both Marcus and Ceionius' son Lucius Verus.

Pius' reign was untroubled, and he governed responsibly and well from 138 to 161, a period of prosperity, senatorial freedom, and relative peace on the frontiers. Meanwhile, Marcus was educated by the most eminent rhetorical and philosophical teachers of his day, and at an early age began to serve under Pius. He was quaestor in 139, consul together with Pius in 140, consul for the second time in 145, and received the tribunician power and proconsular *imperium* (traditional marks of the prospective heir) in 146. In 145 he married Pius' daughter Faustina, and a daughter was born in the following year. Marcus was clearly senior to Lucius Verus (consul only in 154), but upon his accession insisted that they should reign as colleagues, Verus' powers and titles being immediately augmented. Verus' reputation has suffered from much gossip reported in the unreliable *Historia Augusta*, which paints him as a playboy; yet his ties with Marcus were close, and he seems to have been a satisfactory administrator and an adequate general. Verus died in 169.

Marcus himself reigned from 161 to 180. Frontier problems and indeed invasions occupied his attention for many of those twenty years. Britain, Parthia, and especially the many tribes of

the German provinces and the free Germans north of the
Danube all caused recurrent problems, and Marcus campaigned
himself in North Italy and Germany in 168, 170–5 (against the
Marcomanni, the Quadi, and the Sarmatii), and again in Pannonia and Germany from 177 until his death by illness, on campaign near Vienna, in March 180. In 175 he was also hampered
by civil disorder in the empire, following the revolt of Avidius
Cassius, governor of Egypt and Syria. Avidius claimed that news
had reached him of the emperor's death, and the full extent of
his guilt remains doubtful. Scandal implicated Faustina, the
emperor's wife, as Avidius' lover and fellow-conspirator. The
rebellion failed and Avidius was murdered by a centurion; the
historian Dio Cassius presents Marcus' reaction to the revolt as
one of pity, sorrow, and readiness to forgive. Modern readers
have sometimes attempted to find references to this affair, and to
Faustina's supposed infidelities, in the *Meditations*. All such en-
quiries remain speculative, however intriguing. Of Faustina, as
of Verus, he says nothing but good in book i.

Another disaster of Marcus' reign was the plague of 166–7 and
later, apparently brought back from Parthia by Verus' armies. It
is not clear how far this affected the population. Meanwhile,
wars and generous donations of largesse diminished the
treasury's resources dangerously. Bureaucracy and busy official-
dom flourished, but no strong threads of long-term policy can be
readily discerned. Nevertheless, Marcus' lifetime was soon
idealized as a Golden Age, partly because of the violent contrast
provided by the disastrous reign of his son Commodus (born
161, reigned 180–92), who was eventually assassinated and
execrated as a tyrant.

In retrospect, Marcus' reign also arouses interest in modern
readers because of the continuing growth of Christianity (already
familiar and persecuted in the time of Nero, and judiciously
controlled by Trajan). The emperor must have known of the
existence of the cult, but it may still have seemed of little importance at this early date. In the *Meditations* he mentions its
adherents by name only once, with disapproval (xi. 3, in a phrase
which has been doubted as possibly a later gloss); his teacher

Fronto denounced them with the ignorant clichés of polemic; and two episodes of persecution occurred under Marcus' authority and presumably with his knowledge: the martyrdom of the apologist Justin (AD 167?), after a trial conducted by Marcus' close friend Rusticus, and the executions at Lyons in response to a public outcry in 177 (though the date has been questioned).

The *Meditations*, unknown to the authors who describe his reign, were probably written in his last decade. As explained in the main Introduction, they offer exceptional access to the mind of a Roman emperor in a period which is, even by ancient standards, very ill-documented. For narrative accounts of Marcus' life and reign we have to turn to an epitomized portion of Dio Cassius' monumental history of Rome, written in Greek between AD 197 and *c.*225, and to a sketchy biography included in the notoriously unreliable *Historia Augusta* (probably compiled in the late fourth century). The most important contemporary evidence for Marcus' life and character outside the *Meditations* is the fragmentary collection of letters between Marcus and his tutor, Cornelius Fronto (see the Appendix to this volume): these are valuable but badly preserved, and often hard to date. The social, political, and economic background can be further illuminated by public monuments and inscriptions, but it is only in a very few cases that we have reason to suppose that such documents bear much relation to Marcus' own views and words.

FURTHER READING

Texts

C. R. Haines (Loeb Classical Library, Harvard, 1916, with facing translation and useful notes); A. S. L. Farquharson (Oxford, 2 volumes, 1944, with translation and commentary); W. Theiler (Zurich, 1951, with German translation and notes); J. Dalfen (Teubner, Leipzig, 1979, useful for its complete index of words).

Translations

Apart from Haines, Farquharson (used in this volume), and Theiler, the following are worth notice: Meric Casaubon (London, 1634, dedicated to Archbishop Laud; reprinted in Everyman's Library, London, 1906); George Long (London, 1862), singled out for praise by Matthew Arnold in his essay on Marcus; J. Jackson (World's Classics, Oxford, 1906); G. M. A. Grube (Hackett, USA, 1983).

Biography and history

Anthony Birley, *Marcus Aurelius* (Eyre and Spottiswoode, London, 1966; revised edition, Batsford, London, 1987) is the standard biography. E. Champlin, *Fronto and Antonine Rome* (Cambridge Mass., 1980) is important for the emperor's upbringing and for the life of the court.

Three outstanding works on the intellectual and religious background are: E. R. Dodds, *Pagan and Christian in an Age of Anxiety* (Cambridge, 1965); P. Brown, *The World of Late Antiquity* (Thames and Hudson, London, 1971, with fascinating illustrations); A. D. Nock, *Conversion* (Oxford, 1933). Longer and more demanding, but very stimulating, is Robin Lane Fox, *Pagans and Christians* (Harmondsworth, 1986; Penguin edition, 1988). All of these range well beyond Marcus Aurelius' life and writings; a superb modern article on Marcus himself, which has greatly influenced my own approach, is by P. A. Brunt, 'Marcus Aurelius in his *Meditations*', *Journal of Roman Studies*, 64 (1974), 1–20. My own book *The Meditations of Marcus Aurelius: a Study* (Oxford, 1989) is an attempt to combine literary and stylistic criticism of the work with consideration of Marcus' ideas and outlook; whatever its deficiencies, it remains, as far as I know, the only book that does attempt this.

Stoicism

A straightforward guide to the whole history of the school is F. H. Sandbach, *The Stoics* (Chatto and Windus, London, 1975). More advanced is A. A. Long, *Hellenistic Philosophy* (Duckworth, London, 1974), ch. 4. A detailed sourcebook with philosophic commentary on translated passages is now available: A. A. Long and D. N. Sedley, *The Hellenistic Philosophers* (Cambridge, 1987), vol. i, of which pp. 158–437 deal with Stoicism in depth. The second volume of this work contains the Greek and Latin texts of the sources.

For the non-philosopher a much more direct introduction to Roman Stoicism may be had through reading parts of Seneca (especially the *Moral Epistles* and the *On Anger*) and Epictetus (especially the *Handbook* or *Manual*); both these authors are available in the Loeb Classical Library, and there is also a selection from Seneca's *Epistles* in the Penguin Classics, entitled *Seneca: Letters from a Stoic*.

Full details of works cited above are normally not repeated in the notes to the Introduction and Translation.

A NOTE ON THE TEXT

No ancient writer survives in his own original handwriting; in all cases we are dealing with a tradition which transmits the original by one route or many, one stage or many, and in all traditions errors are introduced, either (more commonly) by miscopying, or by deliberate abbreviation, expansion, and 'improvements'. The tradition of the *Meditations* presumably goes back to a single autograph, perhaps preserved by the emperor's family or a faithful secretary. The work seems to have been very little known in later antiquity; the first references to it date from the fourth and the tenth centuries. The lexicon known as the Suda, probably compiled *c*. AD 950, quotes a number of extracts and uses the twelve-book division. But although scholarly interest awakened, it seems that readers were often content with excerpts and selections—not surprisingly, since the author is often repetitive. Knowledge of the *Meditations* was limited until in 1559 Xylander published the first printed edition, using a manuscript (usually called P) which is now lost. Another manuscript of the whole work, known as A, still survives and is to be found in the Vatican; this dates from the late fourteenth or early fifteenth century. Xylander did not know A; the central issue in the textual criticism of Marcus is thus to weigh Xylander (= ?P) against the extant A. There are also a number of manuscripts containing extracts only (fourteenth to sixteenth centuries). This slender tradition makes it unlikely in many passages that we can ever certainly restore Marcus' authentic text; the brevity and allusiveness of his language, and the likelihood that he was writing for himself only, compound the problems. But by the labours of generations of scholars much has been done; in particular, study of Epictetus and other philosophic authors has served to elucidate Marcus' thought and often to confirm and correct his text. The reader of Farquharson's translation can feel fairly confident of finding there, if not a faithful reproduction, at least a fair reflection, of the actual words of Marcus Aurelius.

THE *MEDITATIONS* OF
MARCUS AURELIUS ANTONINUS

BOOK I

1. From* my grandfather Verus:* the lessons of noble character and even temper.

2. From my father's reputation and my memory of him:* modesty and manliness.

3. From my mother:* piety and bountifulness, to keep myself not only from doing evil but even from dwelling on evil thoughts, simplicity too in diet and to be far removed from the ways of the rich.

4. From my mother's grandfather:* not to have attended public schools but enjoyed good teachers at home,* and to have learned the lesson that on things like these it is a duty to spend liberally.

5. From my tutor:* not to become a partisan of the Green jacket or the Blue in the races, nor of Thracian or Samnite gladiators;* to bear pain and be content with little; to work with my own hands, to mind my own business, and to be slow to listen to slander.

6. From Diognetus:* to avoid idle enthusiasms; to disbelieve the professions of sorcerers and impostors about incantations and exorcism of spirits and the like;* not to cock-fight* or to be excited about such sports; to put up with plain-speaking and to become familiar with philosophy; to hear the lectures first of Baccheius, then of Tandasis and Marcian, in boyhood to write essays and to aspire to the camp-bed and skin coverlet and the other things which are part of the Greek training.

7. From Rusticus:* to get an impression of need for reform and treatment of character; not to run off into zeal for rhetoric, writing on speculative themes, discoursing on edifying texts, exhibiting in fanciful colours the ascetic or the philanthropist. To avoid oratory, poetry, and preciosity; not to parade at home in

ceremonial costume or to do things of that kind; to write letters in the simple style, like his own from Sinuessa to my mother. To be easily recalled to myself* and easily reconciled with those who provoke and offend, as soon as they are willing to meet me. To read books accurately and not be satisfied with superficial thinking about things or agree hurriedly with those who talk round a subject. To have made the acquaintance of the *Discourses* of Epictetus,* of which he allowed me to share a copy of his own.

8. From Apollonius:* moral freedom, not to expose oneself to the insecurity of fortune; to look to nothing else, even for a little while, except to reason. To be always the same, in sharp attacks of pain, in the loss of a child, in long illnesses. To see clearly in a living example that a man can be at once very much in earnest and yet able to relax.

Not to be censorious in exposition; and to see a man who plainly considered technical knowledge and ease in communicating general truths as the least of his good gifts. The lesson how one ought to receive from friends what are esteemed favours, neither lowering oneself on their account, nor returning them tactlessly.

9. From Sextus:* graciousness, and the pattern of a household governed by its head, and the notion of life according to Nature. Dignity without pretence, solicitous consideration for friends, tolerance of amateurs and of those whose opinions have no ground in science.

A happy accommodation to every man, so that not only was his conversation more agreeable than any flattery, but he excited the greatest reverence at that very time in the very persons about him. Certainty of grasp, and method in the discovery and arrangement of the principles necessary to human life.

Never to give the impression of anger or of any other passion, but to be at once entirely passionless and yet full of natural affection. To praise without noise, to be widely learned without display.

10. From Alexander the grammarian:* to avoid fault-finding and not to censure in a carping spirit any who employ an exotic phrase, a solecism, or harsh expression, but oneself to use, neatly

and precisely, the correct phrase, by way of answer or confirmation or handling of the actual question—the thing, not its verbal expression—or by some other equally happy reminder.

11. From Fronto:* to observe how vile a thing is the malice and caprice and hypocrisy of absolutism; and generally speaking that those whom we entitle 'Patricians' are somehow rather wanting in the natural affections.

12. From Alexander the Platonist:* seldom and only when absolutely necessary to say to anyone or write in a letter: 'I am too busy'; nor by such a turn of phrase to evade continually the duties incident to our relations to those who live with us, on the plea of 'present circumstances'.

13. From Catulus:* not to neglect a friend's remonstrance, even if he may be unreasonable in his remonstrance, but to endeavour to restore him to his usual temper. Hearty praise, too, of teachers, like what is recorded of Athenodotus and Domitius,* and genuine love towards children.

14. From Severus:* love of family, love of truth, and love of justice. To have got by his help to understand Thrasea, Helvidius, Cato, Dio, Brutus,* and to conceive the idea of a commonwealth based on equity and freedom of speech,* and of a monarchy cherishing above all the liberty of the subject. From him, too, consistency and uniformity in regard for philosophy; to do good, to communicate liberally, to be hopeful; to believe in the affection of friends and to use no concealment towards those who incurred his censure, and that his friends had no necessity to conjecture his wishes or the reverse, but he was open with them.

15. From Maximus:* mastery of self and vacillation in nothing; cheerfulness in all circumstances and especially in illness. A happy blend of character, mildness with dignity, readiness to do without complaining what is given to be done. To see how in his case everyone believed 'he really thinks what he says, and what he does, he does without evil intent'; not to be surprised or alarmed; nowhere to be in a hurry or to procrastinate, not to lack resource or to be depressed or cringing or

on the other hand angered or suspicious. To be generous, forgiving, void of deceit. To give the impression of inflexible rectitude rather than of one who is corrected. The fact, too, that no one would ever have dreamt that he was looked down on by him or would have endured to conceive himself to be his superior. To be agreeable also (in social life).

16.* From my father (by adoption): gentleness and unshaken resolution in judgements taken after full examination; no vainglory about external honours; love of work and perseverance; readiness to hear those who had anything to contribute to the public advantage; the desire to award to every man according to desert without partiality; the experience that knew where to tighten the rein, where to relax. Prohibition of unnatural practices,* social tact and permission to his suite not invariably to be present at his banquets nor to attend his progress from Rome, as a matter of obligation, and always to be found the same by those who had failed to attend him through engagements. Exact scrutiny in council and patience; not that he was avoiding investigation, satisfied with first impressions. An inclination to keep his friends, and nowhere fastidious or the victim of manias but his own master in everything, and his outward mien cheerful. His long foresight and ordering of the merest trifle without making scenes. The check in his reign put upon organized applause and every form of lip-service; his unceasing watch over the needs of the empire and his stewardship of its resources; his patience under criticism by individuals of such conduct. No superstitious fear of divine powers or with man any courting of the public or obsequiousness or cultivation of popular favour, but temperance in all things and firmness; nowhere want of taste or search for novelty.

In the things which contribute to life's comfort, where Fortune was lavish to him, use without display and at the same time without apology, so as to take them when they were there quite simply and not to require them when they were absent. The fact that no one would have said that he was a sophist, an impostor, or a pedant, but a ripe man, an entire man, above flattery, able to preside over his own and his subjects' business.

Besides all this the inclination to respect genuine followers of philosophy, but towards the other sort no tendency to reproach nor on the other hand to be hoodwinked by them; affability, too, and humour, but not to excess. Care of his health in moderation, not as one in love with living nor with an eye to personal appearance nor on the other hand neglecting it, but so far as by attention to self to need doctoring or medicine and external applications for very few ailments.

A very strong point, to give way without jealousy to those who had some particular gift like literary expression or knowledge of the Civil Law or customs or other matters, even sharing their enthusiasm that each might get the reputation due to his individual excellence. Acting always according to the tradition of our forefathers, yet not endeavouring that this regard for tradition should be noticed. No tendency, moreover, to chop and change, but a settled course in the same places and the same practices. After acute attacks of headache, fresh and vigorous at once for his accustomed duties; and not to have many secrets, only very few and by way of exception, and those solely because of matters of State. Discretion and moderation alike in the provision of shows, in carrying out public works, in donations to the populace, and so on; the behaviour in fact of one who has an eye precisely to what it is his duty to do, not to the reputation which attends the doing.

He was not one who bathed at odd hours, not fond of building, no connoisseur of the table, of the stuff and colour of his dress, of the beauty of his slaves. His costume was brought to Rome from his country house at Lorium; his manner of life at Lanuvium; the way he treated the tax-collector who apologized at Tusculum, and all his behaviour of that sort.* Nowhere harsh, merciless, or blustering, nor so that you might ever say 'to fever heat', but everything nicely calculated and divided into its times, as by a leisured man; no bustle, complete order, strength, consistency. What is recorded of Socrates* would exactly fit him: he could equally be abstinent from or enjoy what many are too weak to abstain from and too self-indulgent in enjoying. To be strong, to endure, and in either case to be sober belong to the man of perfect and invincible spirit, like the spirit of Maximus in his illness.*

17. From the gods: to have had good grandparents, good parents, a good sister, good masters, good intimates, kinsfolk, friends, almost everything; and that in regard to not one of them did I stumble into offence, although I had the kind of disposition which might in some circumstances have led me to behave thus; but it was the goodness of the gods that no conjunction of events came about which was likely to expose my weakness. That I was not brought up longer than I was with my grandfather's second wife,* that I preserved the flower of my youth and did not play the man before my time, but even delayed a little longer. That my station in life was under a governor and a father who was to strip off all my pride and to lead me to see that it is possible to live in a palace and yet not to need a bodyguard or embroidered uniforms or candelabra and statues bearing lamps and the like accompaniments of pomp,* but that one is able to contract very nearly to a private station and not on that account to lose dignity or to be more remiss in the duties that a prince must perform on behalf of the public. That I met with so good a brother,* able by his character not only to rouse me to care of myself but at the same time to hearten me by respect and natural affection; that my children were not deficient in mind nor deformed in body; that I made no further progress in eloquence and poetry and those other pursuits wherein, had I seen myself progressing along an easy road, I should perhaps have become absorbed. That I made haste to advance my masters to the honours which they appeared to covet and did not put them off with hopes that, as they were still young, I should do it later on. To have got to know Apollonius, Rusticus, Maximus. To have pictured to myself clearly and repeatedly what life in obedience to Nature really is,* so that, so far as concerns the gods and communications from the other world, and aids and inspirations,* nothing hinders my living at once in obedience to Nature, though I still come somewhat short of this by my own fault and by not observing the reminders and almost the instructions of the gods. That my body has held out so well in a life like mine; that I did not touch Benedicta or

Theodotus,* but that even in later years when I experienced the passion of love I was cured; that though I was often angry with Rusticus I never went to extremes for which I should have been sorry; that though my mother was fated to die young, she still spent her last years with me. That whenever I wanted to help anyone in poverty or some other necessity I was never told that I could not afford it, and that I did not myself fall into the same necessity so as to take help from another; that my wife* is what she is, so obedient, so affectionate, and so simple; that I was well provided with suitable tutors for my children. That I was granted assistance in dreams,* especially how to avoid spitting blood and fits of giddiness, and the answer of the oracle at Caieta: 'Even as thou shalt employ thyself';* and that, although in love with philosophy, I did not meet with any sophist or retire to disentangle literary works or syllogisms or busy myself with problems 'in the clouds'.* For all these things require 'the gods to help and Fortune's hand'.*

BOOK II

*Written among the Quadi on the river Gran**

1. Say to yourself in the early morning:* I shall meet today inquisitive, ungrateful, violent, treacherous, envious, uncharitable men. All these things have come upon them through ignorance* of real good and ill. But I, because I have seen that the nature of good is the right, and of ill the wrong, and that the nature of the man himself who does wrong is akin to my own (not of the same blood and seed, but partaking with me in mind, that is in a portion of divinity),* I can neither be harmed by any of them, for no man will involve me in wrong, nor can I be angry with my kinsman or hate him; for we have come into the world to work together, like feet, like hands, like eyelids, like the rows of upper and lower teeth. To work against one another therefore is to oppose Nature, and to be vexed with another or to turn away from him is to tend to antagonism.

2. This whatever it is that I am, is flesh and vital spirit and the governing self. Disdain the flesh: blood and bones and network, a twisted skein of nerves, veins, arteries. Consider also what the vital spirit is: a current of air, not even continuously the same, but every hour being expelled and sucked in again. There is then a third part, the governing self. Put away your books, be distracted no longer, they are not your portion. Rather, as if on the point of death, reflect like this: 'you are an old man,* suffer this governing part of you no longer to be in bondage, no longer to be a puppet pulled by selfish impulse, no longer to be indignant with what is allotted in the present or to suspect what is allotted in the future.'

3. The work of the gods is full of Providence: the work of Fortune is not divorced from Nature or the spinning and winding of the threads ordained by Providence. All flows from that other world;* and there is, besides, necessity and the well-being of the

whole universe, whereof you are a part. Now to every part of Nature that is good which the nature of the Whole brings, and which preserves that nature; and the whole world is preserved as much by the changes of the compound bodies as by the changes of the elements which compose those bodies. Let this be sufficient for you, these be continually your doctrines. But put away your thirst for books,* that so you may not die murmuring, but truly reconciled and grateful from your heart to the gods.

4. Remember how long you have been putting off these things, and how many times the gods have given you days of grace, and yet you do not use them. Now is it high time to perceive the kind of Universe whereof you are a part and the nature of the governor of the Universe from whom you subsist as an effluence, and that the term of your time is circumscribed, and that unless you use it to attain calm of mind, time will be gone and you will be gone and the opportunity to use it will not be yours again.

5. Each hour be minded, valiantly as becomes a Roman and a man, to do what is to your hand, with precise . . . and unaffected dignity, natural love, freedom and justice; and to give yourself repose from every other imagination. And so you will, if only you do each act as though it were your last, freed from every random aim, from wilful turning away from the directing Reason, from pretence, self-love and displeasure with what is allotted to you. You see how few things a man need master in order to live a smooth and god-fearing life; for the gods themselves will require nothing more of him who keeps these precepts.

6. You are doing yourself violence,* violence, my soul; and you will have no second occasion to do yourself honour. Brief is the life of each of us, and this of yours is nearly ended, and yet you do not reverence yourself, but commit your well-being to the charge of other men's souls.*

7. Do things from outside break in to distract you? Give yourself a time of quiet to learn some new good thing and cease to wander out of your course. But, when you have done that, be on your guard against a second kind of wandering. For those who are sick to death in life, with no mark on which they direct every

impulse or in general every imagination, are triflers, not in words only but also in their deeds.

8. Men are not easily seen to be brought into evil case by failure to consider what passes in another's soul; but they who do not read aright the motions of their own soul are bound to be in evil case.

9. Always remember the following: what the nature of the Whole is; what my own nature; the relation of this nature to that; what kind of part it is of what kind of Whole; and that no man can hinder your saying and doing at all times what is in accordance with that Nature whereof you are a part.

10. Like a true philosopher Theophrastus says,* when comparing, as men commonly do compare, various faults, that errors of appetite are graver than errors of temper. For clearly one who loses his temper is turning away from Reason with a kind of pain and inward spasm; whereas he who offends through appetite is the victim of pleasure and is clearly more vicious in a way and more effeminate in his wrong-doing. Rightly then and in a truly philosophic spirit Theophrastus said that an offence attended with pleasure involves greater censure than one attended with pain. And, generally, the latter resembles more a man who was originally wronged and so is forced by pain to lose his temper; the other has begun it himself and has been impelled to do wrong, carried away by appetite to do what he does.

11. In the conviction that it is possible you may depart from life at once, act and speak and think in every case accordingly. But to leave the company of men is nothing to fear, if gods exist;* for they would not involve you in ill. If, however, they do not exist or if they take no care for man's affairs, why should I go on living in a world void of gods, or void of providence? But they do exist, and they do care for men's lives, and they have put it entirely in a man's power not to fall into real ills; for the rest, if anything were an ill, they would have provided also for this, that it may be in every man's power not to fall into it; (and how could what does not make a man worse make his life worse?) But the nature of the Whole would not have winked at these things

either out of ignorance or because (though it knew of them) it had not the power to guard against them or to put them right; neither would it have made so vast an error, from want of power or skill, as to permit good and ill to befall indifferently, both good and bad men equally. Now death and life, good report and evil report, pain and pleasure, wealth and poverty, these all befall men, good and bad alike, equally, and are themselves neither right nor wrong: they are therefore neither good nor ill.

12. How all things are vanishing swiftly, bodies themselves in the Universe and the memorials of them in Time; what is the character of all things of sense, and most of all those which attract by the bait of pleasure or terrify by the threat of pain or are shouted abroad by vanity, how cheap, comtemptible, soiled, corruptible, and mortal: these are for the faculty of mind to consider. To consider too what kind of men those are whose judgements and voices confer honour and dishonour; what it is to die, and that if a man looks at it by itself and by the separating activity of thought strips off all the images associated with death, he will come to judge it to be nothing else but Nature's handiwork. But if a man fears Nature's handiwork he is a mere child; and yet death is not merely Nature's handiwork, but also her well-being. To consider also how mortal man touches God and through what organ of himself, and when that part of him is in what sort of condition.

13. Nothing is more wretched than the man who goes round and round everything, and, as Pindar says,* 'searches the bowels of the earth', and seeks by conjecture to sound the minds of his neighbours, but fails to perceive that it is enough to abide with the Divinity that is within himself and to do Him genuine service. Now that service is to keep Him unsullied by passion, trifling, and discontent with what comes from God or men. What comes from the Gods is to be revered because of excellence; what comes from men is dear because they are of one kindred with himself; pitiful too sometimes, humanly speaking, by reason of their ignorance of good and ill. This disablement is more grievous than that which robs the eyes of the power to distinguish light from darkness.

14.* Even were you about to live three thousand years or thrice ten thousand, nevertheless remember this, that no one loses any other life than this which he is living, nor lives any other than this which he is losing. Thus the longest and the shortest come to the same thing. For the present is equal for all, and what is passing is therefore equal: thus what is being lost is proved to be barely a moment. For a man could lose neither past nor future; how can one rob him of what he has not got? Always remember, then, these two things: one, that all things from everlasting are of the same kind, and are in rotation; and it matters nothing whether it be for a hundred years or for two hundred or for an infinite time that a man shall behold the same spectacle; the other, that the longest-lived and the soonest to die have an equal loss; for it is the present alone of which either will be deprived, since (as we saw) this is all he has and a man does not lose what he has not got.

15. 'Everything is what you judge it to be.' While the retort made to the Cynic philosopher Monimus* is plain enough, plain too is the use of the saying, if one only take the gist of it, so far as it is true.

16. The soul of a man does violence to itself, first and foremost when it becomes so far as in it lies, a separate growth,* a blain as it were upon the Universe. For to turn against anything that comes to pass is a separation from Nature, by which the natures of each of the rest are severally comprehended. Secondly, when it turns away from any human being or is swept counter to him, meaning to injure him, as is the case with the natures of those who are enraged. It violates itself, thirdly, when it is the victim of pleasure or pain; fourthly, when it acts a part, and says or does anything both feignedly and falsely. Fifthly, when, failing to direct any act or impulse of its own upon a mark, it behaves in any matter without a plan or conscious purpose, whereas even the smallest act ought to have a reference to the end. Now the end of reasonable creatures is this: to obey the rule and ordinance of the most venerable of all cities and governments.*

17. Of man's life, his time is a point, his existence a flux, his

sensation clouded, his body's entire composition corruptible, his vital spirit an eddy of breath, his fortune hard to predict, his fame uncertain. Briefly, all the things of the body, a river; all the things of the spirit, dream and delirium; his life a warfare* and a sojourn in a strange land, his after-fame oblivion. What then can be his escort through life? One thing and one thing only, Philosophy. And this is to keep the spirit within him unwronged and unscathed, master of pains and pleasures, doing nothing at random, nothing falsely and with pretence; needing no other to do aught or to leave aught undone; and moreover accepting what befalls it, that is, what is assigned to it, as coming from the other world* from which it came itself. And in all things awaiting death, with a mind that is satisfied, counting it nothing else than a release of the elements from which each living creature is composed. Now if there is no hurt to the elements themselves in their ceaseless changing each into other, why should a man apprehend anxiously the change and dissolution of them all? For this is according to Nature; and no evil is according to Nature.

BOOK III

Written in Carnuntum*

1. We ought to take into account not only the fact that day by day life is being spent and a smaller balance remaining, but this further point also that, should we live longer, it is at least doubtful whether the intellect will hereafter be the same, still sufficient to comprehend events and the speculation which contributes to the understanding alike of things divine and human. For, if the mind begin to decay, there will be no failure of functions like transpiration, nutrition, sense-impression, and desire; but the right employment of ourselves, precision in regard to the related elements of duty, analysis of the indications of sense, to know just whether the time is come to take leave of life,* and all questions of the kind which specially require a trained judgement—these are extinguished before the rest. Accordingly we must press forward, not only because every day we are drawing nearer to death, but also because the apprehension of events and the ability to adapt ourselves to them begin to wane before the end.

2. We must also observe closely points of this kind, that even the secondary effects of Nature's processes possess a sort of grace and attraction. To take one instance, bread when it is being baked breaks open at some places; now even these cracks, which in one way contradict the promise of the baker's art, somehow catch the eye and stimulate in a special way our appetite for the food. And again figs, when fully mature, gape, and in ripe olives their very approach to decay adds a certain beauty of its own to the fruit. Ears of corn too when they bend downwards, the lion's wrinkled brow, the foam flowing from the boar's mouth, and many other characteristics that are far from beautiful if we look at them in isolation, do nevertheless because they follow from Nature's processes lend those a further ornament

and a fascination. And so, if a man has a feeling for, and a deeper insight into the processes of the Universe, there is hardly one but will somehow appear to present itself pleasantly to him, even among mere attendant circumstances. Such a man also will feel no less pleasure in looking at the actual jaws of wild beasts than at the imitations which painters and sculptors exhibit, and he will be enabled to see in an old woman or an old man a kind of freshness and bloom, and to look upon the charms of his own boy slaves with sober eyes. And many such experiences there will be, not convincing to everyone but occurring to him and to him alone who has become genuinely familiar with Nature and her works.

3. Hippocrates,* after curing many sicknesses, himself fell sick and died. The Chaldean* astrologers foretold the death of many persons, then the hour of fate overtook them also. Alexander, Pompeius, and Julius Caesar, after so often utterly destroying whole towns and slaying in the field many myriads of horse and foot, themselves also one day departed from life. Heraclitus,* after many speculations about the fire which should consume the Universe, was waterlogged by dropsy, poulticed himself with cow-dung, and died. Vermin killed Democritus; another kind of vermin Socrates.* What is the moral? You went on board, you set sail, you have made the port. Step ashore: if to a second life, nothing is void of gods, not even in that other world; but if to unconsciousness, you will cease to suffer pains and pleasures and to be the servant of an earthly vessel as far inferior as that which does it service is superior; for the one is mind and deity, the other clay and gore.

4. Do not waste the balance of life left to you in thoughts about other persons, when you are not referring to some advantage of your fellows—for why do you rob yourself of something else which you might do—I mean if you imagine to yourself what so and so is doing, and why; what he is saying or thinking or planning, and every thought of the kind which leads you astray from close watch over your governing self?

Rather you must, in the train of your thoughts, avoid what is merely casual and without purpose, and above all curiosity and malice; you must habituate yourself only to thoughts about which if someone were suddenly to ask: 'What is in your mind now?', you would at once reply, quite frankly, *this* or *that*; and so from the answer it would immediately be plain that all was simplicity and kindness, the thoughts of a social being, who disregards pleasurable, or to speak more generally luxurious imaginings or rivalry of any kind, or envy and suspicion or anything else about which you would blush to put into words that you had it in your head.

A man so minded, putting off no longer to be one of the elect, is surely a priest and minister of gods, employing aright that which is seated within him, which makes the mere mortal to be unstained by pleasures, unscathed by any pain, untouched by any wrong, unconscious of any wickedness; a wrestler in the greatest contest of all, not to be overthrown by any passion; dyed with justice to the core, welcoming with his whole heart all that comes to pass and is assigned to him; seldom and only under some great necessity and for the common good imagining what another person is saying or doing or thinking. For he has only his own work to realize and he keeps in mind continually what is assigned to him from the Whole; his work he makes perfect, his lot he is convinced is good; for the birth-spirit assigned to every man goes with him and carries him along with it.

Moreover, he remembers that all reasonable beings are akin to himself, and that although to care for all men is in accord with man's nature, he is to cling not to the opinion of all men, but only of men who live in accord with Nature. Indeed, he remembers continually what those who do not so live are like, in their homes and abroad, by night and by day; what manner of men they are, and those with whom they defile themselves. Therefore he takes no account even of the praise of such men— men who are not even acceptable to themselves.

5. Do not act unwillingly nor selfishly nor without self-examination, nor with divergent motives. Let no affectation veneer your thinking. Be neither a busy talker, nor a busybody.

Moreover let the God within be the guardian of a real man, a man of ripe years, a statesman, a Roman,* a magistrate, who has taken his post like one waiting for the Retreat to sound, ready to depart, needing no oath nor any man as witness. And see that you have gladness of face, no need of service from without nor the peace that other men bestow. You should stand upright,* not be held upright.

6. If you discover in the life of man something higher than justice, truth, temperance, fortitude, and generally speaking than your understanding contented with itself, where it presents you behaving by the rule of right, and satisfied with destiny, in what is assigned to you and is not yours to choose; if, I say, you see something higher than this, turn to it with all your heart and enjoy the supreme good now that it is found. But if nothing higher is revealed than the very divinity seated within you, sub-ordinating your private impulses to itself, examining your thoughts, having withdrawn itself, as Socrates used to say,* from the sense-affections, and subordinated itself to the gods and mak-ing men its first care; if you find all else to be smaller and cheaper than this, give no room to anything else, to which when once you incline and turn, you will no longer have the power without a struggle to prefer in honour that which is your own, your peculiar good. For it is not right to set up a rival of another kind to the good of Reason and of the Commonwealth; the praise of the multitude, for example, or place or wealth or pleasurable indulgence. All these, though they appear for a little while to be in accord, suddenly gain the mastery and carry a man away. Do you then, I say, simply and of your own free will, choose the higher and hold fast to that. 'But the higher is what is to our advantage';* if to the advantage of a reasonable being, keep hold of that, but if to the advantage of a mere animate creature, say so and preserve your decision without parade; only see to it that you make a choice that will not betray you.

7. Never value as an advantage to yourself what will force you one day to break your word, to abandon self-respect, to hate, suspect, execrate another, to act a part, to covet anything that

calls for walls or coverings to conceal it. A man who puts first his own mind and divinity, and the holy rites of its excellence, makes no scene, utters no groans, will need neither the refuge of solitude nor the crowded streets. What is most worth while, he will pass his days neither in pursuit nor in avoidance, and it is no concern at all of his whether the time be longer or shorter for which he shall have the use of the soul in its bodily envelope; for even if he must be released at once, he will depart as easily as he would perform any other act that can be done with reverence and sobriety, being careful all his life of this one thing alone that his understanding be not found in any state which is foreign to a reasonable social being.

8. In the understanding of a man of chastened and purified spirit you will find no trace of festering wound, no ulceration, no abscess beneath the skin. The hour of fate does not surprise his life before its fulfilment, so that one would say that the actor is leaving the stage before he has fulfilled his role, before the play is over. You will find nothing servile or artificial, no dependence on others nor severance from them; nothing to account for, nothing that needs a hole to hide in.

9. Reverence your faculty of judgement. On this it entirely rests that your governing self no longer has a judgement disobedient to Nature and to the estate of a reasonable being. This judgement promises deliberateness, familiar friendship with men, and to follow in the train of the gods.

10. Therefore throw all else aside, and hold fast only these few things; further calling to mind at the same time that each of us lives only in the present, this brief moment; the rest is either a life that is past, or is in an uncertain future. Little the life each lives, little the corner of the earth he lives in,* little even the longest fame hereafter, and even that dependent on a succession of poor mortals, who will very soon be dead, and have not learnt to know themselves, much less the man who was dead long years ago.

11. To the above supports let one more be added. Always make a figure or outline of the imagined object as it occurs, in order

to see distinctly what it is in its essence, naked,* as a whole and parts; and say to yourself its individual name and the names of the things of which it was compounded and into which it will be broken up. For nothing is so able to create greatness of mind as the power methodically and truthfully to test each thing that meets one in life, and always to look upon it so as to attend at the same time to the use which this particular thing contributes to a Universe of a certain definite kind, what value it has in reference to the Whole, and what to man, who is a citizen of the highest City, whereof all other cities are like households. What is this which now creates an image in me, what is its composition? how long will it naturally continue, what virtue is of use to meet it; for example, gentleness, fortitude, truth, good faith, simplicity, self-reliance, and the rest? Therefore, in each case, we must say: this has come from God; this by the actual co-ordination of events, the complicated web and similar coincidence or chance; this again from my fellow man, my kinsman, my comrade, yet one who does not know what is natural for himself. But I do know; wherefore I use him kindly and justly, according to the natural law of fellowship, aiming, however, at the same time at his desert, where the question is morally indifferent.

12. If you complete the present work, following the rule of right, earnestly, with all your might, with kindness, and admit no side issue, but preserve your own divinity pure and erect, as if you have this moment to restore it; if you make this secure, expecting nothing and avoiding nothing, but content with present action in accord with Nature and with heroic truth in what you mean and say, you will live the blessed life. Now there is no one who is able to prevent this.

13. As doctors* have their instruments and scalpels always at hand to meet sudden demands for treatment, so do you have your doctrines ready in order to recognize the divine and human, and so to do everything, even the very smallest, as mindful of the bond which unites the divine and human; for you will not do any act well which concerns man without referring it to the divine; and the same is true of your conduct to God.

14. Do not wander from your path any longer, for you are not likely to read your notebooks or your deeds of ancient Rome and Greece or your extracts from their writings,* which you laid up against old age. Hasten then to the goal, lay idle hopes aside, and come to your own help, if you care at all for yourself, while still you may.

15. They* have not learnt to know the manifold significance of theft, of sowing, of buying, resting, seeing what ought to be done. This depends not on the bodily eye but on another kind of vision.

16. Body, vital spirit, mind: of the body, sense perceptions; of the vital spirit, impulses; of the mind, doctrines. To be impressed by images belongs also to the beasts of the field, to be swayed by the strings of impulse to wild beasts, to men who sin against nature,* to a Phalaris* or a Nero. To have the mind as guide to what appear to be duties belongs also to men who do not believe in gods, who betray their own country, who do anything and everything once they have locked their doors.* If then all else is common to you with those whom I have mentioned, it remains the peculiar mark of the good man to love and welcome what befalls him and is the thread fate spins for him; not to soil the divinity seated within his breast nor to disquiet it with a mob of imaginations, but to preserve and to propitiate it, following God in orderly wise, uttering no word contrary to truth, doing no act contrary to justice. And if all men disbelieve that he lives simply, modestly, and cheerfully, he is not angry with any one of them nor diverted from the road that leads to the goal of his life, at which he must arrive, pure, peaceful, ready to depart, in effortless accord with his own birth-spirit.

BOOK IV

1.* The sovereign power within, in its natural state, so confronts what comes to pass as always to adapt itself readily to what is feasible and is presented to it. This is because it puts its affection upon no material of its own choice; rather it sets itself upon its objects with a reservation, and then makes the opposition which encounters it into material for itself. It is like a fire, when it masters what falls into it, whereby a little taper would have been put out, but a bright fire very quickly appropriates and devours what is heaped upon it, and leaps up higher out of those very obstacles.

2. Nothing that is undertaken is to be undertaken without a purpose, nor otherwise than according to a principle which makes the art of living perfect.

3*. Men look for retreats for themselves, the country, the sea-shore, the hills; and you yourself, too, are peculiarly accustomed to feel the same want. Yet all this is very unlike a philosopher, when you may at any hour you please retreat into yourself. For nowhere does a man retreat into more quiet or more privacy than into his own mind, especially one who has within such things that he has only to look into, and become at once in perfect ease; and by ease I mean nothing else but good behaviour. Continually, therefore, grant yourself this retreat and repair yourself. But let them be brief and fundamental truths,* which will suffice at once by their presence to wash away all sorrow, and to send you back without repugnance to the life to which you return.

For what is it that shall move your repugnance? The wickedness of men? Recall the judgement that reasonable creatures have come into the world for the sake of one another; that patience is a part of justice; that men do wrong involuntarily; and how many at last, after enmity, suspicion, hatred, warfare, have been laid out on their death-beds and come to dust.

This should make you pause. But shall what is assigned from Universal Nature be repugnant to you? Revive the alternative: 'either Providence or blind atoms',* and the many proofs that the Universe is a kind of Commonwealth. Shall then the things of the flesh still have hold upon you? Reflect that the understanding, when once it takes control of itself and recognizes its own power, does not mingle with the vital spirit, be its current smooth or broken, and finally reflect upon all that you have heard and consented to about pain and pleasure.

Well, then, shall mere glory distract you? Look at the swiftness of the oblivion of all men; the gulf of endless time, behind and before; the hollowness of applause, the fickleness and folly of those who seem to speak well of you, and the narrow room in which it is confined. This should make you pause. For the entire earth is a point in space, and how small a corner thereof is this your dwelling place, and how few and how paltry those who will sing your praises here!

Finally, therefore, remember your retreat into this little domain which is yourself, and above all be not disturbed nor on the rack, but be free and look at things as a man, a human being, a citizen,* à creature that must die. And among what is most ready to hand into which you will look have these two: the one, that things do not take hold upon the mind, but stand without unmoved, and that disturbances come only from the judgement within; the second, that all that your eyes behold will change in a moment and be no more; and of how many things you have already witnessed the changes, think continually of that.

The Universe is change, life is opinion.

4. If mind is common to us all, then also the reason, whereby we are reasoning beings, is common. If this be so, then also the reason which enjoins what is to be done or left undone is common. If this be so, law also is common; if this be so, we are citizens; if this be so, we are partakers in one constitution; if this be so, the Universe is a kind of Commonwealth. For in what other common government can we say that the whole race of men partakes? And thence, from this common City, is derived our mind itself, our reason and our sense of law, or from what else?

For as the earthy is in me a portion from some earth, and the watery from a second element, and the vital spirit from some source, and the hot and fiery from yet another source of its own (for nothing comes from nothing, just as nothing returns to nothing), so therefore the mind also has come from some source.

5. Death is like birth, a mystery of Nature; a coming together out of identical elements and a dissolution into the same. Looked at generally this is not a thing of which man should be ashamed, for it is contrary neither to what is conformable to a reasonable creature nor to the principle of his constitution.

6. These are natural and necessary results from creatures of this kind, and one who wants this to be otherwise wants the fig-tree* not to yield its acrid juice. And in general remember this, that within a very little while both he and you will be dead, and a little after not even your name nor his will be left.

7. Get rid of the judgement; you are rid of the 'I am hurt'; get rid of the 'I am hurt', you are rid of the hurt itself.

8. What does not make a man worse than he was, neither makes his life worse than it was, nor hurts him without or within.

9. It was a law of necessity that what is naturally beneficial should bring this about.

10. 'All that comes to pass comes to pass with justice.' You will find this to be so if you watch carefully. I do not mean only in accordance with the ordered series of events, but in accordance with justice and as it were by someone who assigns what has respect to worth. Watch, therefore, as you have begun and whatever you do, do it with this, with goodness in the specific sense in which the notion of the good man is conceived. Preserve this goodness in everything you do.

11. Don't regard things in the light in which he who does the wrong judges them, nor as he wishes you to judge them: but see them as in truth they are.

12. In these two ways you must always be prepared: the one, only to act as the principle of the royal and law-giving art*

prescribes for the benefit of mankind; the second, to change your purpose, if someone is there to correct and to guide you away from some fancy of yours.* The guidance must, however, always be from a conviction of justice or common benefit ensuing, and what you prefer must be similar, not because it looked pleasant or popular.

13. 'You have reason?' 'Yes, I have?' 'Why not use it then? If this is doing its part, what else do you want?'

14. You came into the world as a part. You will vanish in that which gave you birth, or rather you will be taken up into its generative reason by the process of change.*

15. Many grains of incense upon the same altar; one falls first, another later, but difference there is none.*

16. Within ten days you will appear a god even to those* to whom today you seem a beast or a baboon, if you return to your principles and your reverence of the Word.

17. Don't live as though you were going to live a myriad years. Fate is hanging over your head; while you have life, while you may, become good.

18. How great a rest from labour he gains who does not look to what his neighbour says or does or thinks,* but only to what he himself is doing, in order that exactly this may be just and holy, or in accord with a good man's conduct. 'Do not look round at a black character',* but run towards the goal, balanced, not throwing your body about.

19. The man in a flutter for after-fame fails to picture to himself that each of those who remember him will himself also very shortly die, then again the man who succeeded him, until the whole remembrance is extinguished as it runs along a line of men who are kindled and then put out. And put the case that those who will remember never die, and the remembrance never dies, what is that to you! And I do not say that it is nothng to the dead; what is praise to the living, except perhaps for some practical purpose? For now you are putting off unseasonably the gift of Nature, which does not depend on the testimony of some one else . . .*

20. Everything in any way lovely is of itself and terminates in itself, holding praise to be no part of itself. At all events, in no case does what is praised become better or worse. This I say also of what is commonly called lovely, for instance materials and work of art; and indeed what is there lacking at all to that which is really lovely? No more than to law, no more than to truth, no more than to kindness or reverence of self. Which of these is lovely because it is praised or corrupted because it is blamed? Does an emerald become worse than it was, if it be not praised? And what of gold, ivory, purple, a lute, a sword-blade, a flower-bud, and little plant?

21. You ask how, if souls continue to exist,* the atmosphere has room for them from time eternal. But how does the ground have room for the bodies of those who for so long an age are buried in it? The answer is that, as on earth change and dissolution after a continuance for so long make room for other dead bodies, so in the atmosphere souls pass on and continue for so long, and then change and are poured out and are kindled being assumed into the generative principle of Universal Nature, and so provide room for those which succeed to their place. This would be the answer presuming that souls do continue. But we must consider not only the multitude of bodies that are thus buried, but also the number of animals eaten every day by ourselves and the rest of the animal creation. How large a number are devoured and in a manner of speaking buried in the bodies of those who feed upon them; and yet there is room to contain them because they are turned into blood, because they are changed into forms of air and heat. How shall we investigate the truth of this? By a distinction into the material and the causal.

22. Do not wander without a purpose, but in all your impulses render what is just, and in all your imaginations preserve what you apprehend.

23.* Everything is fitting for me, my Universe, which fits thy purpose. Nothing in thy good time is too early or too late for me; everything is fruit for me which thy seasons, Nature, bear; from thee, in thee, to thee are all things. The poet sings: 'Dear city of Cecrops',* and will you not say: 'Dear city of God'?

24. Democritus has said: 'Do few things, if you would enjoy tranquillity'.* May it not be better to do the necessary things and what the reason of a creature intended by Nature to be social prescribes, and as that reason prescribes? For this brings not only the tranquillity from doing right but also from doing few things. For if one removes most of what we say and do as unnecessary, he will have more leisure and less interruption. Wherefore on each occasion he should remind himself: 'Is this *not* one of the necessary things?' And he should remove not actions merely that are unnecessary, but imaginations also, for in this way superfluous actions too will not follow in their train.

25. Make trial for yourself how the life of the good man, too, fares well, of the man pleased with what is assigned from Universal Nature and contented by his own just action and kind disposition.

26. You have seen those things, look now at these: do not trouble yourself, make yourself simple. Does a man do wrong? He does wrong to himself. Has some chance befallen you? It is well; from Universal Nature, from the beginning, all that befalls was determined for you and the thread was spun.* The sum of the matter is this: life is short; the present must be turned to profit with reasonableness and right. Be sober without effort.

27. Either an ordered Universe or a medley heaped together mechanically but still an order; or can order subsist in you and disorder in the Whole! And that, too, when all things are so distinguished and yet intermingled and sympathetic.*

28. A black heart is* an unmanly heart, a stubborn heart; resembling a beast of prey, a mere brute, or a child; foolish, crafty, ribald, mercenary, despotic.

29. If he is a foreigner* in the Universe who does not recognize the essence of the Universe, no less is he a foreigner, who does not recognize what comes to pass in it. A fugitive is he who runs away from the reasonable law of his City; a blind man,

he who shuts the eye of the mind; a beggar, he who has need of another and has not all that is necessary for life in himself; a blain on the Universe, he who rebels and separates himself from the reason of our common nature because he is displeased with what comes to pass (for Nature who bore you, brings these things also into being); a fragment cut off from the City, he who cuts off his own soul from the soul of reasonable creatures, which is one.

30. Here is a philosopher without a tunic,* another without a book, another here half-naked. 'I have no bread,' he says, 'still I stand firm by the Word.' And I have nourishment from my lessons and yet do not stand firm.

31. Love the art which you were taught, set up your rest in this. Pass through what is left of life as one who has committed all that is yours, with your whole heart, to the gods, and of men making yourself neither despot nor servant to any.

32.* Call to mind by way of example the time of Vespasian: you will see everything the same: men marrying, bringing up children, falling ill, dying, fighting, feasting, trading, farming, flattering, asserting themselves, suspecting, plotting, praying for another's death, murmuring at the present, lusting, heaping up riches, setting their heart on offices and thrones. And now that life of theirs is no more and nowhere.

Again pass on to the time of Trajan; again everything the same. That life, too, is dead. In like manner contemplate and behold the rest of the records of times and whole nations; and see how many after their struggles fell in a little while and were resolved into the elements. But most of all you must run over in mind those whom you yourself have known to be distracted in vain, neglecting to perform what was agreeable to their own constitution, to hold fast to this and to be content with this. And here you are bound to remember that the attention paid to each action has its own worth and proportion; only so you will not be dejected if in smaller matters you are occupied no farther than was appropriate.

33. Words familiar in olden times are now archaisms; so also the names of those whose praises were hymned in bygone days

are now in a sense archaisms;* Camillus, Caeso, Volesus, Dentatus;* a little after, Scipio too and Cato; then also Augustus, then also Hadrian and Antoninus. For all things quickly fade and turn to fable, and quickly, too, utter oblivion covers them like sand. And this I say of those who shone like stars to wonder at; the rest, as soon as the breath was out of their bodies, were 'unnoticed and unwept'.* And what after all is everlasting remembrance? Utter vanity. What then is that about which a man ought to spend his pains? This one thing;* right understanding, neighbourly behaviour, speech which would never lie, and a disposition welcoming all which comes to pass, as necessary, as familiar, as flowing from a source and fountain like itself.

34. With your whole will surrender yourself to Clotho to spin your fate into whatever web of things she will.

35.* All is ephemeral, both what remembers and what is remembered.

36. Contemplate continually all things coming to pass by change, and accustom yourself to think that Universal Nature loves nothing so much as to change what is and to create new things in their likeness. For everything that is, is in a way the seed of what will come out of it, whereas you imagine seeds to be only those which are cast into the earth or into the womb. But that is very unscientific.*

37. You will presently be dead and are not yet simple, untroubled, void of suspicion that anything from outside can hurt you, not yet propitious to all men, nor counting wisdom to consist only in just action.

38. Look into their governing principles, even the wise among them, what petty things they avoid and what pursue!

39. Your evil does not consist in another's governing principle, nor indeed in any change and alteration of your environment. Where then? Where the part of you which judges about evil is. Let it not frame the judgement, and all is well. Even if what is nearest to it, your body, is cut, cauterized, suppurates, mortifies, still let the part which judges about these things be at rest; that

is, let it decide that nothing is good or evil which can happen indifferently to the evil man and the good. For what happens indifferently to one whose life is contrary to Nature and to one whose life is according to Nature, this is neither according to nor contrary to Nature.

40. Constantly think of the Universe as one living creature, embracing one being and one soul; how all is absorbed into the one consciousness of this living creature; how it compasses all things with a single purpose, and how all things work together to cause all that comes to pass, and their wonderful web and texture.

41. You are a spirit bearing the weight of a dead body, as Epictetus used to say.*

42. For what comes to pass in the course of change nothing is evil, as nothing is good for what exists in consequence of change.

43. There is a kind of river of things passing into being, and Time is a violent torrent.* For no sooner is each seen, then it has been carried away, and another is being carried by, and that, too, will be carried away.

44. All that comes to pass is as familiar and well known as the rose in spring and the grape in summer. Of like fashion are sickness, death, calumny, intrigue, and all that gladdens or saddens the foolish.

45. What follows is always organically related to what went before; for it is not like a simple enumeration of units separately determined by necessity, but a rational combination; and as Being is arranged in a mutual co-ordination, so the phenomena of Becoming display no bare succession but a wonderful organic interrelation.

46. Always remember what Heraclitus said:* 'the death of earth is the birth of water, the death of water is the birth of atmosphere, the death of atmosphere is fire, and conversely'. Remember, too, his image of the man who forgets the way he is going; and: 'they are at variance with that with which they most continuously have converse (Reason which governs the Universe),

and the things they meet with every day appear alien to them';
and again: 'we must not act and speak like men who sleep, for
in sleep we suppose that we act and speak'; and 'we must not be
like children with parents', that is, accept things simply as we
have received them.

47. Just as, if one of the gods told you: 'tomorrow you will be
dead or in any case the day after tomorrow', you would no longer
be making that day after important any more than tomorrow,
unless you are an arrant coward (for the difference is a mere trifle), in the same way count it no great matter to live to a year that
is an infinite distance off rather than till tomorrow.

48. Think continually how many physicians have died, after
often knitting their foreheads over their patients; how many
astrologers after prophesying other men's deaths, as though to
die were a great matter; how many philosophers after endless
debate on death or survival after death; how many paladins after
slaying their thousands; how many tyrants after using their
power over men's lives with monstrous arrogance, as if
themselves immortal; how many entire cities have,* if I may use
the term, died, Helice, Pompeii, Herculaneum, and others in-
numerable. Run over, too, the many also you know of, one after
another. One followed this man's funeral and then was himself
laid on the bier; another followed him, and all in a little while.
This is the whole matter: see always how ephemeral and cheap
are the things of man—yesterday, a spot of albumen,* tomorrow,
ashes or a mummy. Therefore make your passage through this
span of time in obedience to Nature and gladly lay down your
life, as an olive, when ripe, might fall, blessing her who bare it
and grateful to the tree which gave it life.

49. Be like the headland on which the waves continually
break, but it stands firm and about it the boiling waters sink to
sleep. 'Unlucky am I, because this has befallen me.' Nay rather:
'Lucky am I, because, though this befell me, I continue free from
sorrow, neither crushed by the present, nor fearing what is to
come.' For such an event might have befallen any man, but not
every man would have continued in it free from sorrow. On what

grounds then is this ill fortune more than that good fortune? Do you, speaking generally, call what is not a deviation from man's nature a man's ill fortune, and do you suppose that what is not opposed to his natural will is a deviation from his nature? Very well, you have been taught what that will is. Can what has befallen you prevent your being just, high-minded, temperate, prudent, free from rash judgements, trustful, self-reverent, free, and whatever else by its presence with him enables a man's nature to secure what is really his? Finally, in every event which leads you to sorrow, remember to use this principle: that this is not a misfortune, but that to bear it like a brave man is good fortune.

50. An unscientific but none the less a helpful support to disdain of death is to review those who have clung tenaciously to life. What more did they gain than those who died prematurely? In every case they are laid in some grave at last: Caedicianus, Fabius, Julianus, Lepidus,* and any others like them, who after carrying many to the grave were themselves carried out. To speak generally the difference is a small one, and this difference long-drawn-out through what great toils and with what sorts of men and in how weak a body. Do not count it then as a thing . . .; for see the gulf of time behind and another infinite time in front: in this what difference is there between a three-days-old infant and a Nestor of three generations?

51. Run always the short road, and Nature's road is short. Therefore say and do everything in the soundest way, because a purpose like this delivers a man from troubles and warfare, from every care and superfluity.

BOOK V

1. At dawn of day, when you dislike being called,* have this thought ready: 'I am called to man's labour; why then do I make a difficulty if I am going out to do what I was born to do and what I was brought into the world for? Is it for this that I am fashioned, to lie in bedclothes and keep myself warm?' 'But this is more pleasant.' 'Were you born then to please yourself; in fact for feeling, not for action? Can't you see the plants, the birds, the ants,* the spiders, the bees each doing his own work, helping for their part to adjust a world? And then you refuse to do a man's office and don't make haste to do what is according to your own nature.' 'But a man needs rest as well.' I agree, he does, yet Nature assigns limits to rest, as well as to eating and drinking, and you nevertheless go beyond her limits, beyond what is sufficient; in your actions only this is no longer so, there you keep inside what is in your power. The explanation is that you do not love your own self, else surely you would love both your nature and *her* purpose. But other men who love their own crafts wear themselves out in labours upon them, unwashed and unfed; while you hold your own nature in less honour than the smith his metal work, the dancer his art, the miser his coin, the lover of vainglory his fame. Yet they, when the passion is on them, refuse either to eat or to sleep sooner than refuse to advance the objects they care about, whereas you imagine acts of fellowship to bring a smaller return and to be deserving of less pains.

2. How simple to reject and to wipe away every disturbing or alien imagination, and straightway to be in perfect calm.

3. Make up your mind that you deserve every word and work that is according to Nature, and do not allow the ensuing blame or speech of any men to talk you over; but, if it is right to be done or said, do not count yourself undeserving of it. Those others have their own selves to govern them, and use their several

inclinations. Don't look round at that, but walk the straight way, following your own and the common Nature, for the path of them both is one.

4. I walk in Nature's way until I shall lie down and rest, breathing my last in this from which I draw my daily breath, and lying down on this from which my father drew his vital seed, my mother her blood, my nurse her milk; from which for so many years I am fed and watered day by day; which bears my footstep and my misusing it for so many purposes.

5. 'Your mental powers they cannot admire.' Granted! but there is much else of which you cannot say: 'that is no gift of mine'. Bring forth then what is wholly in your power, freedom from guile, dignity, endurance of labour, distaste for pleasure, contentment with your portion, need of little, kindness, freedom, plain-living, reserve in speech, magnanimity. See you not how much you are able to bring forth, where there is no excuse of want of gift or want of facility, and yet you are content to keep a lower place? Are you obliged to grumble, to be grasping, to flatter, to blame your poor body, to be obsequious, to vaunt yourself, to tossed about in mind, because you have been fashioned without talent? No, by heaven, you had the power to be rid of all this long ago, and only, if at all, to be convicted of some slowness and tardiness of understanding; and even there you should exercise yourself, not disregarding your faults nor finding satisfaction in your dullness.

6. One kind of man, when he does a good turn to someone, is forward also to set down the favour to his account. Another is not forward to do this, but still within himself he thinks as though he were a creditor and is conscious of what he has done. A third is in a sense not even conscious of what he has done, but he is like a vine which has borne grapes, and asks nothing more when once it has borne its appropriate fruit. A horse runs, a hound tracks, bees make honey, and a man does good, but doesn't know that he has done it* and passes on to a second act, like a vine to bear once more its grapes in due season. You ought then to be one of these who in a way are not aware of what they do. 'Yes,

but one ought to be aware precisely of this; for', he argues, 'it is a mark of the social being to perceive it too.' What you are saying is true, but you take what is now meant in the wrong way; because of this you will be one of those whom I mentioned above, for they, too, are led astray by a kind of plausible reasoning. But if you make up your mind to understand what is meant, do not be afraid of omitting thereby any social act.'

7. A prayer of the people of Athens:* 'Rain, beloved Zeus, rain on the cornfields and the plains of Attica.' One ought to pray thus simply and freely, or not to pray at all.

8. We commonly say: 'Aesculapius* ordered a man horse-exercise, cold baths, or no shoes'; similarly we might say: 'Universal Nature ordered him sickness, disablement, loss or some other affliction.' In the former phrase 'ordered' virtually means 'laid this down for him as appropriate to health'; in the latter what befits every man has been laid down for him as appropriate to the natural order. So, too, we say things 'befit us' as workmen talk of squared blocks 'fitting' in walls or pyramids bonding with one another in a definite structure. For in the whole of things there is one connecting harmony, and as out of all material bodies the world is made perfect into a connected body, so out of all causes the order of Nature is made perfect into one connected cause. Even quite simple folk have in their minds what I am saying, for they use the phrase; 'it was sent to him'; and so this was 'sent' to him, that is, 'this was ordered for him'. Accordingly let us accept these orders as we accept what Aesculapius orders. Many of them, too, are assuredly severe, yet we welcome them in hopes of health. Let the performance and completion of the pleasure of the Universal Nature seem to you to be your pleasure, precisely as the conduct of your health is seen to be, and so welcome all that comes to pass, even though it appear rather cruel, because it leads to that end, to the health of the universe, that is to the welfare and well-being of Zeus. For he would not 'send' this to one, if it were not to the well-being of the whole, no more than any living principle you may choose 'sends' anything which is not appropriate to what is governed

by it. Thus there are two reasons why you must be content with what happens to you: first because it was for you it came to pass, for you it was ordered and to you it was related, a thread of destiny stretching back to the most ancient causes; secondly because that which has come to each individually is a cause of the welfare and the completion and in very truth of the actual continuance of that which governs the Whole. For the perfect Whole is mutilated if you sever the least part of the contact and continuity alike of its causes as of its members; and you do this so far as in you lies, whenever you are disaffected, and in a measure you are destroying it.

9. Don't be disgusted, don't give up, don't be impatient if you do not carry out entirely conduct based in every detail upon right principles; but after a fall return again, and rejoice if most of your actions are worthier of human character. Love that to which you go back, and don't return to Philosophy as to a schoolmaster, but as a man with sore eyes to the sponge and salve, as another to a poultice, another to a fomentation. For so you will show that to obey Reason is no great matter but rather you will find rest in it. Remember, too, that philosophy wills nothing else than the will of your own nature, whereas you were willing some other thing not in accord with Nature. For what is sweeter than this accord? Does not pleasure overcome us just by sweetness? Well, see whether magnanimity, freedom, simplicity, consideration for others, holiness are not sweeter; for what is sweeter than wisdom itself when you bear in mind the unbroken current in all things of the faculty of understanding and knowledge?

10. Realities are so veiled, one might say, from our eyes that not a few and those not insignificant thinkers* thought them to be incomprehensible, while even the Stoics think them difficult of comprehension; and all our assent to perceptions is liable to alter. For where is the infallible man to be met? Pass on, then, to objects of experience—how short their duration, how cheap, and able to be in the possession of the bestial,* the harlot, or the brigand. Next pass to the characters of those who live with you, even the best of whom it is hard to suffer, not to say that it is

hard for a man even to endure himself. In such a fog and filth,*
in so great a torrent of being and time and movement and moving
things, what can be respected or be altogether the object of
earnest pursuit I do not see. On the contrary, one must console
oneself by awaiting Nature's release, and not chafing at the circumstances of delay, but finding repose only in two things: one,
that nothing will befall me which is not in accordance with the
nature of the Whole; the other, that it is in my power to do
nothing contrary to my God and inward Spirit; for there is no
one who shall force me to sin against this.

11. 'To what purpose, then, am I now using my soul?' In
every case ask yourself this question and examine yourself: 'What
have I now in this part which men call the governing part, and
whose soul have I at present? A child's, a boy's, a woman's, a
despot's, a dumb animal's, a dangerous beast's?'

12. You could apprehend the character of what the majority
of men fancy to be 'goods' like this. If a man were to conceive
the existence of real goods, like wisdom, temperance, justice, fortitude, he could not with those in his mind still listen to the
popular proverb about 'goods in every corner', for it will not fit.
But with what appear to the majority of men to be goods in his
mind he will listen to and readily accept what the comic poet*
said as an appropriate witticism. In this way even the majority
perceive the difference, otherwise this proverb would not in the
one case offend and be disclaimed, whereas in the case of wealth
and the blessings which lead to luxury or show we accept it as
a witticism to fit the case. Go on, then, and ask whether one
should respect and conceive to be good, things to which when
one has thought of them one could properly apply the proverb
that their owner is so well off that he 'has not a corner where to
ease himself'.

13. I was composed of a formal and a material substance; and
of these neither will pass away into nothingness, just as neither
came to exist out of nothingness. Thus, every part of me will be
assigned its place by change into some part of the Universe, and
that again into another part of the Universe, and so on to infinity.

By a similar change both my parents and I came to exist, and so on to another infinity of regression. For there is no reason to prevent one speaking so, even if the Universe is governed according to finite periods (of coming to be and passing away).*

14. Reason and the method of reasoning are abilities, sufficient to themselves and their own operations. Thus, they start from their appropriate principle and proceed to their proposed end; wherefore reasonable acts are called right acts, to indicate the rightness of their path.

15. A man ought to treasure none of these things, which does not fall to a man's portion *qua* man. They are not requirements of a man, nor does man's nature profess them, nor are they accomplishments of man's nature. Accordingly man's end does not lie in them, and certainly not the good which is complementary to his end. Moreover, if any of these were given as his portion to man, it would not have been his portion to disdain them and to resist them, nor would the man who made himself independent of them have been laudable nor the man who took less of them than he might, have been good, if they were really 'goods'. But as things are, the more a man robs himself of these and other such, the more he forbears when he is robbed of them, so much the more is he good.

16. As are your repeated imaginations so will your mind be, for the soul is dyed by its imaginations.* Dye it, then, in a succession of imaginations like these: for instance, where it is possible to live, there also it is possible to live well: but it is possible to live in a palace, therefore it is also possible to live well in a palace.* Or once more: a creature is made for that in whose interest it was created: and that for which it was made, to this it tends: and to what it tends, in this is its end: and where its end is, there is the advantage and the good alike of each creature: therefore fellowship is the good of a reasonable creature. For it has been proved long ago* that we are born for fellowship; or was it not plain that the inferior creatures are in the interests of the superior, the superior of one another? But the animate are

superior to the inanimate and the reasoning to the merely animate.

17. To pursue the impossible is madness: but it is impossible for evil men not to do things of this sort.

18. Nothing befalls anything which that thing is not naturally made to bear. The same experience befalls another, and he is unruffled and remains unharmed; either because he is unaware that it has happened or because he exhibits greatness of soul.* Is it not strange that ignorance and complaisance are stronger than wisdom . . .?

19. Things as such do not touch the soul in the least: they have no avenue to the soul nor can they turn or move it. It alone turns and moves itself, and it makes what is submitted to it resemble the judgements of which it deems itself deserving.

20.* In one relation man is the nearest creature to ourselves, so far as we must do them good and suffer them. But so far as they are obstacles to my peculiar duties, man becomes something indifferent to me as much as sun or wind or injurious beast. By these some action might be hindered, but they are not hindrances to my impulse and disposition, because of my power of reservation and adaptation; for the understanding adapts and alters every obstacle to action to suit its object, and a hindrance to a given duty becomes a help, an obstacle in a given path a furtherance.

21. Reverence the sovereign power over things in the Universe; this is what uses all and marshals all. In like manner, too, reverence the sovereign power in yourself; and this is of one kind with that. For in you also this is what uses the rest, and your manner of living is governed by this.

22. What is not injurious to the city* does not injure the citizens either. On the occasion of every imagination that you have been injured apply this canon: 'If the city is not injured by this neither am I injured.' But if the city is injured you must not be angry, only point out to him who injured the city what he has failed to see.

23. Repeatedly dwell on the swiftness of the passage and departure of things that are and of things that come to be. For substance is like a river in perpetual flux,* its activities are in continuous changes, and its causes in myriad varieties, and there is scarce anything which stands still, even what is near at hand; dwell, too, on the infinite gulf of the past and the future, in which all things vanish away. Then how is he not a fool who in all this is puffed up or distracted or takes it hardly, as if he were in some lasting scene, which has troubled him for long?

24. Call to mind the whole of Substance of which you have a very small portion, and the whole of time whereof a small hair's breadth has been determined for you, and of the chain of causation whereof you are how small a link.

25. Another does wrong. What is that to me? Let him look to it; he has his own disposition, his own activity. I have now what Universal Nature wills me to have, and I do what my own nature wills me to do.

26. See that the governing and sovereign part of your soul is undiverted by the smooth or broken movement in the flesh, and let it not blend therewith, but circumscribe itself, and limit those affections within the (bodily) parts. But when they are diffused into the understanding by dint of that other sympathy,* as needs must be in a united system, then you must not try to resist the sensation, which is natural, yet the governing part must not of itself add to the affection the judgement that it is either good or bad.

27. 'Live with the gods.' But he is living with the gods who continuously exhibits his soul to them, as satisfied with its dispensation and doing what the deity, the portion of himself* which Zeus has given to each man to guard and guide him, wills. And this deity is each man's mind and reason.

28. Are you angry with the man whose person or whose breath is rank?* What will anger profit you? He has a foul mouth, he has foul armpits; there is a necessary connexion between the effluvia and its causes. 'Well, but the creature has reason, and

can, if he stops to think, understand why he is offensive.' Bless you! and so too have you reason; let reasonable disposition move reasonable disposition;* point it out, remind him; for if he hearkens, you will cure him and anger will be superfluous. You are neither play-actor nor harlot.

29. As you intend to live when you depart, so you are able to live in this world; but if they do not allow you to do so, then depart this life, yet so as if you suffered no evil fate. The chimney smokes* and I leave the room. Why do you think it a great matter? But while no such reason drives me out, I remain a free tenant and none shall prevent me acting as I will, and I will what agrees with the nature of a reasonable and social creature.

30.* The mind of the Whole is social. Certainly it has made the inferior in the interests of the superior and has connected the superior one with another. You see how it has subordinated, co-ordinated, and allotted to each its due and brought the ruling creatures into agreement one with another.

31.* How have you hitherto borne yourself to gods, parents, brother, wife, children, masters, tutors, friends, connexions, servants? Has your relation to all men hitherto been: 'not to have wrought nor to have said a lawless thing to any'?* Remind yourself of the kinds of things you have passed through and the kinds you have had strength to endure; that the story of your life is written and your service accomplished.* How many beautiful things have been revealed, how many pleasures and pains you have looked down upon, how many ambitions ignored, to how many unkind persons you have been kind!

32. Why do the ignorant and unlearned confound men of knowledge and learning? What soul has knowledge and learning? That which knows the beginning and end and the reason which informs the whole substance and through all eternity governs the Whole according to appointed cycles.

33. In how short a time, ashes or a bare anatomy, and either a name or not even a name; and if a name, then a sound and an echo.* And all that is prized in life empty, rotten, and petty;

puppies biting one another, little children quarrelling, laughing, and then soon crying. And Faith, Self-respect, Right, and Truth 'fled to Olympus from the spacious earth'.* What, then, still keeps one here, if the sensible is everchanging,* never in one stay, the senses blurred and subject to false impressions; the soul itself an exhalation from blood, and a good reputation in such conditions vanity? What shall we say? Wait in peace, whether for extinction or a change of state;* and until its due time arrives, what is sufficient? What else than to worship and bless the gods, to do good to men, to bear them and to forbear;* and, for all that lies within the limits of mere flesh and spirit, to remember that this is neither yours nor in your power?

34. You are able always to have a favourable tide, if you are able to take a right path, if, that is, you are able both to conceive and to act with rectitude. These two things are common to God's soul and to man's, that is, to the soul of every reasonable creature: not to be subject to another's hindrance, to find his good in righteous act and disposition, and to terminate his desire in what is right.

35. If this is neither evil of mine nor action which results from evil of mine, and if the Universe is not injured, why am I troubled because of it? And what injury is there to the Universe?

36. Don't be carried away by imagination which sees only the surface, but help men as best you may and as they deserve, even though their loss be of something indifferent. Do not, however, imagine the loss to be an injury, for that habit is bad. Like the old man who,* when he went away, used to ask for his foster-child's top, but did not forget that it was a top; so you should act also in this instance. And so you are lamenting in the pulpit!* Have you forgotten, my friend, what these things were worth? 'I know, but to the sufferers* they were of vast importance.' Is that a reason why you should make a fool of yourself too?

37. 'There was a time when I was fortune's favourite, wherever and whenever she visited me.' Yes, but to be fortune's favourite meant assigning good fortune to yourself; and good fortune means good dispositions of the soul, good impulses, good actions.

BOOK VI

1. The matter of the Whole is docile and adaptable, and the Reason that controls it has in its own nature no ground to create evil, for it contains no evil; nor does it create anything amiss nor is any injury done by it; and all things come into being and are accomplished according to it.

2. Provided you are doing your proper work it should be indifferent to you whether you are cold or comfortably warm, whether drowsy or with sufficient sleep, whether your report is evil or good, whether you are in the act of death or doing something else. For even that wherein we die is one of the acts of life,* and so even at that moment to 'make the best use of the present' is enough.

3. Look to what is within: do not allow the intrinsic quality or the worth of any one fact to escape you.

4. All things that exist will very swiftly change; either they will pass into vapour, if we presume that matter is a whole, or else they will be dispersed into their atoms.*

5. The controlling Reason knows its own disposition, what it creates, and the material upon which it works.

6. The noblest kind of retribution is not to become like your enemy.

7. Rejoice and set up your rest in one thing: to pass from act to act of fellowship, keeping God in remembrance.

8. The governing principle it is which wakes itself up and adapts itself, making itself of whatever kind it wills and making all that happens to it appear to be of whatever kind it wills.

9. All things are being accomplished in each case according to the nature of the Whole; for certainly they cannot be in accord-

ance with any other nature, whether embracing them without, or enclosed within, or attached to them outside.

10.* Either a medley, a mutual interlacing of atoms and their scattering: or unification, order, providence. If then the former, why do I so much as desire to wear out my days in a world compounded by accident and in a confusion governed by chance? Why am I concerned about anything else than how I am in one way or another to 'return to earth'?* And why am I troubled? Whatever I do, the scattering into atoms will come upon me. But, if the alternative be true, I bow my head, I am calm, I take courage in that which orders all.

11. Whenever you are obliged by circumstances to be in a way troubled, quickly return to yourself, and do not, more than you are obliged, fall out of step; for you will be more master of the measure by continually returning to it.

12. Had you a step-mother and a mother at the same time, you would wait upon the former but still be continually returning to your mother. This is now what the palace* and your philosophy are to you. Return to her again and again, and set up your rest in her, on whose account that other life appears tolerable to you and you tolerable in it.*

13. Surely it is an excellent plan, when you are seated before delicacies and choice foods, to impress upon your imagination that this is the dead body of a fish, that the dead body of a bird or a pig; and again, that the Falernian wine is grape juice and that robe of purple a lamb's fleece dipped in a shell-fish's blood; and in matters of sex intercourse,* that it is attrition of an entrail and a convulsive expulsion of mere mucus. Surely these are excellent imaginations, going to the heart of actual facts and penetrating them so as to see the kind of things they really are. You should adopt this practice all through your life, and where things make an impression which is very plausible, uncover their nakedness, see into their cheapness, strip off the profession on which they vaunt themselves. For pride is an arch-seducer of reason, and just when you fancy you are most certainly busy in

good works, then you are most certainly the victim of imposture. Consider for instance what Crates says even about Xenocrates.*

14. Most of the objects which the vulgar admire may be referred to the general heads of what is held together by 'stress',* like minerals and timber, or by 'growth', like figs, vines, olives; those admired by slightly superior folk to things held together by 'animal spirit', for instance flocks and herds or bare ownership of a multitude of slaves; those by persons still more refined to things held together by 'reasonable spirit', not, however, reasonable as such but so far as to be technical or skilled in something else. But one who reveres spirit in its full sense of reasonable and political regards those other objects no longer, but above all continually keeps his own spirit in reasonable and social being and activity, co-operating with a fellow being to this end.

15. Some things are hastening to be, others to have come and gone, and a part of what is coming into being is already extinct. Flux and change renew the world incessantly, as the unbroken passage of time makes boundless eternity ever young. In this river,* therefore, on which he cannot stand, which of these things that race past him should a man greatly prize? As though he should begin to set his heart on one of the little sparrows that fly past, when already it has gone away out of his sight. Truly the life of every man is itself as fleeting as the exhalation of spirit from his blood or the breath he draws from the atmosphere. For just as it is to draw in a single breath and to return it, which we do every moment, so is it to render back the whole power of respiration, which you acquired but yesterday or the day before, at birth, to that other world from which you first drew it in.

16. To transpire like plants* or to breathe like cattle or wild beasts is not a thing to value, nor to be stamped by sense impression or drawn by the strings of impulse, nor to live in herds or to take in nourishment—this last is on a level with relieving the body of the dregs of that nourishment. What, then, should be valued?* The clapping of hands? Surely not; and so not even the clapping of tongues, for the applause of multitudes is a clapping

of tongues. Therefore you have put mere glory away. What is left to be valued? To my thinking to move and to be held back according to man's proper constitution, the end to which both rustic industries and the arts give the lead. (For every art aims at this, that what it fashions should be suited to the purpose for which it has been fashioned. This is the aim of the gardener and of the vinedresser, of the breaker of colts and the trainer of dogs.) And to what end do children's training and teaching labour? Here, then, is what is of true value, and if this be well, you will not endeavour to obtain for yourself any one of the rest. Will you not cease to value many other things besides? Then you will not be free or self-contained or passionless; for you will be obliged to entertain envy and rivalry, to regard with suspicion those who are able to take away those things, to plot against those who have what is valued by you. To sum up, he who feels the want of any one of those things must be sullied thereby and besides must often blame the gods. But to reverence and value your own understanding will make you acceptable to yourself, harmonious with your fellows, and in concord with the gods; that is, praising whatsoever they assign and have ordained.

17. The motions of the Elements are up, down, in circles: the movement of man's excellence is in none of these, but proceeding in a more divine way and on a path past finding out it fares well.

18. Only think what it is they do. They refuse to speak good of men living at the same time and in their company, yet themselves set great store on being spoken well of by those who will be born after them, whom they have never seen and never will see. Yet this is next door to being sad because men born before you were not speaking good words about you.

19. Do not because a thing is hard for you yourself to accomplish, imagine that it is humanly impossible: but if a thing is humanly possible and appropriate, consider it also to be within your own reach.

20. In the field a player may have scratched us with his nails or given us a blow with his head, in a rage, yet we do not label

him for that or hit back or suspect him afterwards of designs against us. Still, we do, in fact, keep away from him, not, however, as a foe and not with suspicion but with good-natured avoidance. Let us take this for an example in other departments of life; let us overlook much in the case of those who are, so to speak, our opponents in the game; for, as I said, it is possible to avoid them, yet neither to suspect nor hate them.

21. Suppose a man can convince me of error and bring home to me that I am mistaken in thought or act; I shall be glad to alter, for the truth is what I pursue, and no one was ever injured by the truth, whereas he is injured who continues in his own self-deception and ignorance.

22. Let me do my own duty; nothing else distracts me, for it is either lifeless or without reason or has gone astray and is ignorant of the true path.

23. Use dumb animals and lifeless things and objects generally with a generous and free spirit, because you have reason and they have not; use men because they have reason, in a neighbourly spirit; and in all things call upon for gods for help.* Let it make no difference to you for how long a time you will do these things, for even three hours in this spirit is enough.

24.* Alexander the Great and his stable boy were levelled in death, for they were either taken up into the same life-giving principles of the Universe or were scattered without distinction into atoms.*

25. Reflect upon the multitude of bodily and mental events taking place in the same brief time, simultaneously in every one of us; and so you will not be surprised that many more events, or rather all things that come to pass, exist simultaneously in the one and entire unity, which we call the Universe.

26.* Suppose a man puts you the problem how to write the name Antoninus. Will you raise your voice to pronounce each of its component parts? Then suppose they are angry, will you be angry in return? Will you not quietly enumerate and go over in succession each of the letters? In the same way then, in our life here, remember that every duty has its complement of definite numbers. These you must preserve and not be troubled, and if men make difficulties, not meet them with difficulties, but bring what you propose to do methodically to completion.

27. How inhuman it is to forbid men to set out after what appears suitable and advantageous to themselves. Yet, in a way, you are not allowing them to do this, whenever you are indignant because they do wrong; for certainly they are moved to what looks to be suitable and advantageous to themselves. 'But it is, in fact, not so.' Very well, instruct them and make it plain; don't be indignant.

28. Death is repose from sense-response, from the stimulus of impulse, from intellectual analysis and the service of the flesh.

29. It is absurdly wrong that, in this life where your body does not give in, your spirit should be the first to surrender.

30. Take heed not to be transformed into a Caesar,* not to be dipped in the purple dye; for it does happen. Keep yourself therefore, simple, good, pure, grave, unaffected, the friend of justice, religious, kind, affectionate, strong for your proper work. Wrestle to continue to be the man Philosophy wished to make you. Reverence the gods, save men. Life is brief; there is one harvest of earthly existence, a holy disposition and neighbourly acts. In all things like a pupil of Antoninus;* his energy on behalf of what was done in accord with reason, his equability everywhere, his serene expression, his sweetness, his disdain of glory, his ambition to grasp affairs.

Also how he let nothing at all pass without first looking well into it and understanding it clearly; how he would suffer those who blamed him unjustly, not blaming them in return; how he was in no hurry about anything; how he refused to entertain slander; how exactly he scrutinized men's characters and actions, was not given to reproach, not alarmed by rumour, not suspicious, not affecting to be wise; how he was content with little, in lodging, in his bed, in dress, in food, in service; how he loved work and was long-suffering.

What a man, too, he was to remain in his place until evening; because of his spare diet not needing even to relieve nature except at his usual hour. Moreover, his constancy and uniformity to his friends, his tolerance of plain-spoken opposition to his opinions and delight when anyone indicated a better course; and how he revered the gods without superstition. So may your last hour find you, like him, with a conscience void of reproach.

31. Be sober once more, recall yourself and shake off sleep again. Perceive that they were dreams which troubled you, and once again fully awake, look at these things as you looked at those.

32. I am composed of body and spirit.* Now to the body all things are indifferent, for it cannot distinguish them itself. And to the understanding* all that are not its own activities are indifferent, and all that are its own activities are in its control. Even of these, however, it is concerned only about the present, for its future and past activities are themselves also at the present moment indifferent.

33. Neither pain of hand nor pain of foot is contrary to Nature, provided the foot is doing the service of a foot or the hand of a hand. It follows that not even for a man, as man, is pain contrary to Nature, while he is doing the service of a man, and if pain for him is not contrary to Nature, neither is it an evil for him.

34. What monstrous pleasures brigands, pathics, parricides, and despots enjoy.

35. Do you not see how mechanic craftsmen suit themselves up to a point to amateurs, yet none the less stick to the rule of their craft and never submit to desert that? Is it not grievous, then, that architect and physician will reverence, each the principle of his art, more than man his own principle,* which he has in common with the gods?

36. Asia and Europe are corners in the Universe; every sea, a drop in the Universe; Mount Athos, a clod of earth in the Universe; every instant of time, a pin-prick of eternity. All things

are petty, easily changed, vanishing away. All things come from that other world, starting from that common governing principle, or else are secondary consequences of it. Thus, even the lion's jaws,* deadly poison, and every injurious thing, like a thistle or a bog, are by-products* from those august and lovely principles. Do not, then, imagine them to be contrary to what you reverence, but reflect upon the fountain of all things.

37.* He who sees what is now has seen all things, whatsoever came to pass from everlasting and whatsoever shall be unto unlimited time. For all things are of one kin and of one kind.

38. Meditate often upon the bond of all in the Universe and their mutual relationship. For all things are in a way woven together and all are because of this dear to one another; for these follow in order one upon another because of the stress-movement* and common spirit and the unification of matter.

39. Fit yourself into accord with the things in which your portion has been cast, and love the men among whom your lot has fallen, but love them truly.

40. Every instrument, tool, and vessel is well off, if it carry out the work for which it was fashioned. Yet here the maker is outside the tool. Where things are held together by a natural principle, the power which made them is within and abides with them. You must accordingly reverence it the more, and believe that if you are and continue according to the will of that power, you have all things to your mind. And in like manner its things are to the mind of the All.

41. Should you propose to yourself as good or evil something beyond your will, the necessary result is that, if you fall into that evil or fail of that good, you blame the gods and you hate men who are or who you suspect will be the causes of your loss of the good or your falling into the evil; and indeed we commit many wrongs from concern in regard to these things, If, however, we decide that only what our will controls is good or evil, then no ground is left either to arraign God or to adopt the position of an enemy to man.

42. We are all working together to a single end, some consciously and with understanding, some without knowledge, as Heraclitus,* I think, says that even 'Sleepers are workers and fellow-workers in what comes to pass in the world'. One helps in one way, one in another, and *ex abundanti* even he who finds fault and tries to resist or destroy what is coming to pass; for the Universe has need even for such a one. Finally, therefore, see with which you take your post, for in any event he who controls the whole will employ you aright and will accept you as one part of the fellow-labourers and fellow-workers; only do not you become as mean a part as the cheap and ridiculous verse in the comedy, which Chrysippus* mentions.

43. Does the Sun god claim to do the work of the god of rain, or Aesculapius the work of the Fruit-bearing goddess?* And how is it with each of the stars? Is not their province different, but they are working together to the same end?

44.* If so be that the gods took counsel about me and what must happen to me, they took counsel for good; for it is not easy to conceive a god without purpose, and on what possible ground would be likely to desire to do me harm? What advantage would there be from this either for themselves or for the common good, which is their principal care? But if they took no counsel about me as an individual, surely they did for the common good, and as the present follows upon that by way of consequence, I am bound to welcome and to love it. But suppose they take counsel, if you will, about nothing (a thing it is impious to believe, or else let us cease to sacrifice* and pray to them, to swear by them and to do all else that we do, believing them to be present and living in our midst);* yet still, suppose they take council about none of our concerns, I am able to take counsel about myself, and my consideration is about what is advantageous. Now the advantage of each is what is proper to his own constitution and nature, and my nature is reasonable and social. As Antoninus, my city and my fatherland is Rome; as a man, the Universe.* All then that benefits these cities is alone my good.

45. All that befalls the individual is to the advantage of the

Whole. This should be enough. However, if you watch carefully, you will generally see this besides: what advantages a man also advantages the rest of men; but here advantage must be taken in its more usual acceptance* of what lies in between good and evil.

46. Just as the performances in the amphitheatre* and such places pall upon you, being for ever the same scenes, and the similarity makes the spectacle nauseating, so you feel in the same way about life as a whole; for all things, up and down, are the same and follow from the same. How long will it last?*

47.* Think constantly of the death of men of all sorts, of all sorts of pursuits and of every kind of nation, so that your thought comes down to Philistio, Phoebus, and Origanio. Now pass on to the remaining classes of men. We are bound to change to that other world, where are so many subtle orators, so many grave philosophers, Heraclitus, Pythagoras, and Socrates; so many heroes of old, captains and kings of later days. Besides these, Eudoxus, Hipparchus, and Archimedes, other acute natures, great minds, hard workers, rogues, self-willed men, those who made mock of man's mortal and transient life itself, like Menippus and all of his kind.* Of them all reflect that long ago they were laid in the ground. Why was it dreadful for them, why dreadful for those whose names are not even remembered? One thing here is of great price, to live out life with truth and righteousness, gracious to liars and to the unrighteous.

48.* Whenever you desire to cheer yourself, think upon the merits of those who are alive with you; the energy of one, for instance, the modesty of another, the generosity of a third, of another some other gift. For nothing is so cheering as the images of the virtues shining in the character of contemporaries, and meeting so far as possible in a group. Therefore you should keep them ready to your hand.

49. You are not discontented, surely, because you weigh only so many pounds and not three hundred? So, too, because you may only live so many years and no longer? As you are contented

with the quantity of matter determined for you, so also be contented with your days.

50. Endeavour to persuade them, but act even if they themselves are unwilling, when the rule of justice so directs. If, however, a man employs force to resist, change your object to resignation and freedom from a sense of present injury, and use the opposition to elicit in yourself a different virtue. Remember, too, that you set out with a reservation* and were not aiming at the impossible. What then was your aim? 'An aim qualified by a reservation.' But you do achieve this; what we proposed to ourselves does come to pass.

51. He who loves glory thinks the activity of another to be his own good; he who loves pleasure thinks his own feeling to be his good; he who has intelligence, thinks his own action to be his good.

52. It is possible to entertain no thought about this, and not be troubled in spirit; for things of themselves are not so constituted as to create our judgements upon them.

53.* Habituate yourself not to be inattentive to what another has to say and, so far as possible, be in the mind of the speaker.

54. What does not benefit the hive is no benefit to the bee.

55. If the crew spoke evil of the master of the ship* or his patients of the doctor, would they listen to any one else? Or how should the master achieve safety for the passengers or health for those he is treating?

56. How many in whose company I came into the world are gone away already!

57. Honey appears bitter to the jaundiced, water is dreaded by those bitten by a mad dog, and to little boys a ball seems a fine thing. Why then am I angry? Or do you think that misrepresentation has smaller power over men than bile over the jaundiced or poison over the victim of a bite?

58. No one will prevent your living by the rule of your own

nature: nothing will happen to you contrary to the rule of Universal Nature.

59. What creatures they are whom they wish to please, and by what kind of results and what kind of actions! How swiftly eternity will cover all things, and how many it has covered already!

BOOK VII

1. This is Evil; it is that which you have often seen. Have this ready to hand at every emergency, that this is what you have often seen. You will in general find the same things repeated up and down the world. The ancient chronicles are full of them, those of the middle age, the recent. Cities and households today are full of them. There is nothing new, all alike familiar and short-lived.

2. Your principles are living principles.* How else can they become lifeless, except the images which tally with them be extinguished? And with you it lies to rekindle them constantly. 'I am able to think as I ought about this; if, then, I am able, why am I troubled? Things outside my understanding are nothing at all in regard to my understanding.' Master this, and you stand upright. To come back to life is in your power; look once more at things as once you did, for herein to come back to life consists.

3.* A procession's vain pomp, plays on a stage, flocks, herds, sham fights, a bone thrown to puppies, a crumb into fishponds, toiling and moiling of ants carrying their loads, scurrying of startled mice, marionettes dancing to strings. Well, then, you must stand up in all this, kindly and not carrying your head proudly; yet understand that every man is worth just so much as the worth of what he has set his heart upon.

4. In conversation one ought to follow closely what is being said; in the field of impulse to follow what is happening; in the latter case to see immediately what is the object of reference, in the former to mark closely the meaning expressed.

5. Is my understanding sufficient for this or not? If it is sufficient, I employ it for the task as an instrument bestowed on me by Universal Nature. But if it is insufficient, either I withdraw* from the task in favour of one who can accomplish it better

(provided in other ways this is my duty), or else I do it as best I can, taking to help me one who by using my intelligence to assist him can do what is now opportune and beneficial for the general public. For whatever I do, by myself or with another, should contribute solely to this, the general benefit and harmony.

6. How many whose praises have been loudly sung are now committed to oblivion: how many who sang their praises are long ago departed.

7. Do not be ashamed to be helped; the task before you is to accomplish what falls to your lot, like a soldier in a storming-party.* Suppose you are lame and cannot scale the wall by yourself, yet it can be done with another's help.

8. Let not the future trouble you; for you will come to it, if come you must, bearing with you the same reason which you are using now to meet the present.

9. All things are woven together and the common bond is sacred, and scarcely one thing is foreign to another, for they have been arranged together in their places and together make the same ordered Universe. For there is one Universe out of all, one God through all, one substance and one law, one common Reason of all intelligent creatures and one truth, if indeed the perfection of creatures of the same family and partaking of the same Reason is one.

10. Everything material vanishes very swiftly in the Universal Substance, every cause is very swiftly taken up into the Universal Reason, and the memorial of everything is very swiftly buried in eternity.

11. For a reasonable creature the same act is according to Nature and according to Reason.

12.* Upright, or held upright.

13.* Reasonable beings, constituted for one fellowship of co-operation, are in their separated bodies analogous to the several members of the body in individual organisms. The idea of this will come home to you more if you say to yourself: 'I am a member of the system made up of reasonable beings.' If, however, by the change of one letter, you call yourself a part, you do not yet love men from your heart; well-doing is not yet a joy to you for its own sake; you are still doing it as a bare duty, not yet as though doing good to yourself.

14. Let what will from outside happen to what can be affected by this happening, for the parts which are affected shall, if they please, find fault; whereas I myself, unless I conceive the accident to be evil, am not yet harmed; and it is my power not to conceive it to be evil.

15. Whatever any one may do or say, I am bound to be good; exactly as if gold or emerald or purple were continually to say this: 'whatever any one may do or say, I am bound to be an emerald and to keep the colour that is mine.'

16. The governing self does not create disorder for itself; I mean, for instance, it does not alarm itself or lead itself to appetite. If, however, anyone else can alarm it or give it pain, let him do so, for it will not itself, with the consent of its judgement, turn to such moods. Let the body, if it can, be careful itself to suffer nothing; and the vital spirit which entertains fear and grief, if it suffers anywhere, let it say that it does; but that which delivers judgement generally on these affections will not suffer, for it will not itself be hasty to deliver such a judgement. The governing power regarded by itself has no wants, unless it create want for itself, and in the same way it is untroubled and unhindered, unless it trouble and hinder itself.

17. Happiness is a good genius or a good familiar spirit. 'What then are you doing here, phantom of imagination? Depart, in God's name, the way you came; I have no need of you. But you have come according to your ancient habit. I am not angry with you, only depart.'

18. Is it change that a man fears? Why, what can have come to be without change, and what is dearer or more familiar to Universal Nature? Can you yourself take your bath, unless the

firewood changes? Can you be nourished, unless what you eat changes? Can any other service be accomplished without change? Do you not see that it is precisely your changing which is similar, and similarly necessary to Universal Nature?

19. Through the matter of the Whole, as through a winter torrent, all bodies are passing, connatural with the Whole and co-operating with it, as our members work with one another. How many a Chrysippus,* a Socrates, an Epictetus has Eternity already sucked down! Let the same thought strike you in the case of any single individual or object.

20. One thing only troubles me, that I may not myself do something which the constitution of man does not intend, or in the way it does not intend, or which at this moment it does not intend.

21. Near at hand is your forgetting all; near, too, all forgetting you.

22. It is a property of man to love even those who stumble.* This feeling ensues if it occur to you at the time that men are your kindred and go wrong because of ignorance* and against their will; that in a little while both of you will be dead; but, above all, that he did you no harm, for he did not make your governing self worse than it was before.

23. Universal Nature out of its whole material, as from wax, models now the figure of a horse, then melting this down uses the material for a tree, next for a man, next for something else. And these, every one, subsist for a very brief while. Yet it is no hardship for a box to be broken up, as it was none for it to be nailed together.

24. A scowl on the face is eminently against Nature and, whenever it is often repeated, the expression dies or is at last extinguished, so that it loses the power to light up again. . . . Try to understand this very point that it is against Reason. For if even the consciousness of doing wrong has gone,* what ground for living is left?

25. Everything that your eyes look upon will be changed almost in a moment by Nature which orders the Whole, and out of the material it will create other things, and again out of their material others, in order that the world may be ever fresh and young.*

26. When a man offends against you, think at once what conception of good or ill it was which made him offend. And, seeing this, you will pity him,* and feel neither surprise nor anger. For you yourself still conceive either the same object as he does to be good, or something else of the same type; you are bound, therefore, to excuse him. If, on the other hand, you no longer conceive things of that kind to be goods or ills, you will the more easily be kind to one whose eye is darkened.

27. Do not think of what are absent as though they were not existing, but ponder on the most fortunate of what you have got, and on account of them remind yourself how they would have been missed, if they had not been here. Take heed at the same time not to accustom yourself to overvalue the things you are thus contented to have, so as to be troubled if at any time they are *not* here.

28. Withdraw into yourself:* the reasonable governing self is by its nature content with its own just actions and the tranquillity it thus secures.

29*. Wipe away the impress of imagination. Stay the impulse which is drawing you. Define the time which is present. Recognize what is happening to yourself or another. Divide and separate the event into its causal and material aspects. Dwell in thought upon your last hour. Leave the wrong done by another where the wrong arose.

30. Direct your thought to what is being said. Let your mind gain an entrance into what is occurring and who is producing it.

31. Make yourself glad in simplicity, self-respect, and indifference to what lies between virtue and vice. Love mankind. Follow God. Democritus* says: 'All (sensibles) are ruled by law,

but in reality the elements alone exist.' Enough for you to remember that '*all* exist by law'; now is there very little else.

32. On Death: either dispersal, if we are composed of atoms; or if we are a living unity, either extinction or a change of abode.

33. On Pain: What we cannot bear removes us from life; what lasts can be borne.* The understanding, too, preserves its own tranquillity by abstraction, and the governing self does not grow worse; but it is for the parts which are injured by the pain, if they can, to declare it.

34. On Fame: see what their minds are like, what they avoid, what pursue. And, besides, that as the sands are constantly carried over one another, hiding what went before, so in our life what was before is very swiftly hidden by what is carried after.

35.* 'Do you really imagine that an intelligence endowed with greatness of heart and a vision of all time and all reality thinks this mortal life to be a great thing?' 'Impossible', was his answer. 'Then such a man as that will consider even death not a thing to be dreaded, will he not?' 'Most assuredly.'

36.* 'A King's part: to do good and to be reviled.'

37. It is absurd* that a man's expression should obey and take a certain shape and fashion of beauty at the bidding of the mind, whereas the mind itself is not shaped and fashioned to beauty by itself.

38.* 'Man must not vent his passion on dead things,
       Since they care nothing. . . .'

39.* 'May it be joy that you give to the immortal gods and to men.'

40.* 'Life, like ripe corn, must to the sickle yield,
       And one must be, another cease to be.'

41.* 'Were the gods careless of my sons and me,
       Yet there is reason here.'

42.* 'For with me stand both Righteousness and Good.'

43.* 'Mourn not with them that sorrow; feel no thrill.'

44.* 'But I should have a right answer to give him, as follows: "You speak unadvisedly, my friend, if you fancy that a man who is worth anything ought to take the risk of life or death into account, and not to consider only one thing, when he is acting, whether he does what is right or wrong, the actions of a good man or a bad." '

45.* 'For really and truly, men of Athens, the matter stands like this: wherever a man takes post, believing it to be the best, or is posted by his captain, there he ought, as I think, to remain and abide the risk, taking into account nothing, whether death or anything else, in comparison with dishonour.'

46.* 'But consider, my friend, whether possibly high spirit and virtue are not something other than saving one's life and being saved. Perhaps a man who is really a man must leave on one side the question of living as long as he can, and must not love his life, but commit these things to God, and, believing the women's proverb that no one ever escaped his destiny, must consider, with that in his mind, how he may live the best possible life in the time that is given him to live.'

47.* Watch and see the courses of the stars as if you ran with them, and continually dwell in mind upon the changes of the elements into one another; for these imaginations wash away the foulness of life on the ground.

48.* Moreover, when discoursing about mankind, look upon earthly things below as if from some place above them—herds, armies, farms, weddings, divorces, births, deaths, noise of law courts, lonely places, divers foreign nations, festivals, mournings, market places, a mixture of everything and an order composed of contraries.

49. Behold the past, the many changes of dynasties; the future, too, you are able to foresee, for it will be of like fashion, and it is impossible for the future to escape from the rhythm of the present. Therefore to study the life of man for forty years is no dif-

ferent from studying it for a hundred centuries. For what more
will you see?

50.* 'The earth-born parts return to earth again,
      But what did blossom of ethereal seed
      Returns again to the celestial pole.'
Or else this: an undoing of the interlacement of the atoms and
a similar shattering of the senseless molecules.

51.* 'With gifts of meat and drink and magic charms
      Turning aside the current not to die.'

      'Man must endure whatever wind doth blow
      From God, and labour still without lament.'

52. 'A better man at wrestling': but not more sociable or more
modest or better trained to meet occasion or kinder to the fault
of neighbours.

53. Where work can be accomplished according to the reason
which is common to gods and men, there is nothing to fear; for
where it is possible to obtain benefit by action which moves on
an easy path and according to your constitution, there is no injury to suspect.

54. Everywhere and continually it is in your power to be
reverently content with your present circumstance, to behave to
men who are present with you according to right and to handle
skilfully the present impression, that nothing you have not
mastered may cross the threshold of the mind.

55. Do not look round to the governing selves of men different
from yourself, but keep looking straight forward to the goal to
which Nature is leading you, Universal Nature through what
befalls you, and your own nature by what has to be done by
yourself. Now each must do what follows from its constitution,
and while the other creatures are constituted for the sake of the
reasonable (just as in all else the inferior are for the sake of the
superior),* the reasonable are for one another's sake. Thus the
principal end in man's constitution is the social; and the second,
to resist the passions of the body; for it is a property of reasonable
and intelligent movement to limit itself and never to be worsted

by movements of sense or impulse; for each of those belong to the animal in us, but the movement of intelligence resolves to be sovereign and not to be mastered by those movements outside itself. And rightly so, for that is constituted by nature to make use of them. The third end in a reasonable constitution is to avoid rash judgement and not to be deceived. Let the governing self, therefore, hold fast to these, and progress on a straight path, and it possesses what is its own.

56. As though you were now dead and have not lived your life up to the present moment, use the balance remaining to live henceforward according to Nature.

57. Love only what falls to your lot and is destined for you; what is more suited to you than that?

58. On each occurrence keep before your eyes those to whom the same happened, and then they were sorry, were surprised, complained. And now where are they? Nowhere. Very well, do you, too, desire what they desired? Will you not leave the moods of others to those who shift their moods and are shifted, and yourself be entirely concerned with the way to treat them? For you will treat them well and they will be material* for yourself; only attend and resolve to be fair to yourself in all that you do, and call both things to your mind that what you do is important and that it is unimportant in what sphere your action lies.

59.* Delve within; within is the fountain of good, and it is always ready to bubble up, if you always delve.

60.* The body, too, should be composed, not sprawling about, whether in motion or in repose. For we should require of the body as a whole just what the mind exhibits in the face, when it preserves it intelligent and comely. But all these precautions must be adopted without affectation.

61. The art of living resembles wrestling more than dancing, in as much as it stands prepared and unshaken to meet what comes and what it did not foresee.

62. Constantly stop and consider the manner of men these are

whose testimony you desire to gain, and their ruling principles; for, if you look into the sources of their judgement and impulse, you will not blame those who stumble involuntarily nor will you invite their testimony to yourself.

63. 'No soul is willing to be robbed of truth,' he says.* The same holds of justice, too, of temperance, of kindness, and the like. It is most necessary to remember this continually, for thus you will be more gentle to all men.

64. In the case of every pain be ready with the reflection that it is not an evil, and does not injure the intelligence at the helm; for it does not destroy it, in so far as the soul is reasonable and social. In the case of most pains, however, the saying of Epicurus should help you: 'Pain is neither intolerable nor continuing, provided you remember its limits and do not let your imagination add to it.'* Remember, too, that many disagreeable feelings are identical with pain, and yet we do not perceive that they are; drowsiness, for example, and extreme heat, and loss of appetite. Whenever, then, you are disgusted in one or other of these ways, say to yourself: 'you are giving in to pain.'

65. See that you do not feel to the inhuman what they feel to mankind.

66. How do we know that Telauges* was not in character superior to Socrates? It is not enough that Socrates won more glory by his death, argued more fluently with the Sophists, spent the whole frosty night* in the open with more endurance, thought it braver to refuse, when ordered to arrest Leo of Salamis,* and 'carried his head high in the streets'* (a trait in regard to which one might question whether it was true). No, we have to consider this: what kind of soul Socrates had, whether he could be content with being just in his dealings with men and righteous in his dealing with the gods, whether he was neither hastily indignant with wickedness nor a servant to any man's ignorance, whether he neither accepted as unfamiliar anything assigned by Universal Nature or endured it as intolerable, nor submitted his mind to be affected by the affections of the flesh.

67. Nature did not so blend you with the compound Whole that she did not permit you to circumscribe yourself and to bring what is its own into submission to itself. Always bear this in mind, and further that to live the blessed life rests upon very few conditions; and do not, just because you have abandoned hope of being a thinker and a student of science, on this account despair of being free, modest, sociable, and obedient to God; for it is possible to become an entirely godlike man and yet not to be recognized by anyone.

68. Live out your life without restraint in entire gladness even if all men shout what they please against you, even if wild beasts tear in pieces the poor members of this lump of matter that has hardened about you. For, in the midst of all this, what hinders the mind from preserving its own self in tranquillity, in true judgement about what surrounds it and ready use of what is submitted to it, so that judgement says to what befalls it: 'this is what you are in reality, even if you seem other in appearance', and use says to what is given to it: 'I was looking for you, for the present is to me always material of reasonable and political virtue, that is (generally speaking) of the art of man or God'; since whatever comes to pass is suited to God or man, and is neither novel nor hard to deal with, but familiar and easy to handle.

69. Perfection of character possesses this: to live each day as if the last, to be neither feverish nor apathetic, and not to act a part.*

70. The gods, who have no part in death, are not grieved because in so long an eternity they will be obliged always and entirely to suffer so many and such worthless men; and besides they take care of them in all kinds of ways.* Yet do you, who are all but at the point of vanishing, give up the struggle, and that though you are one of the worthless?

71. It is ridiculous not to flee from one's own wickedness, which is possible, but to flee from other men's wickedness, which is impossible.

72. Whatever the reasonable and political faculty discovers to be neither intelligent nor social, with good reason it decides to be beneath itself.

73.* When you have done good and another has been its object, why do you require a third thing besides, like the foolish—to be thought to have done good or to get a return?

74. No one wearies of receiving benefits, and to benefit another is to act according to Nature. Do not weary then of the benefits you receive by the doing of them.

75. The Universal Nature felt an impulse to create a world; and now either everything that comes into being arises by way of necessary consequence,* or even the sovereign ends to which the ruling principle of the world directs its own impulse are devoid of reason. To remind yourself of this will make you calmer in the face of many accidents.

BOOK VIII

1. This also conduces to contempt of vainglory, that it is no longer in your power to have lived your whole life, or at any rate your life from manhood, in the pursuit of philosophy. To yourself as well as to many others it is plain that you fall far short of philosophy. And so you are tainted, and it is no longer easy for you to acquire the reputation of a philosopher. Your calling, too,* in life has a rival claim. Therefore, if you have truly seen where the matter at issue lies, put away the question of what men will think of you and be satisfied if you live the rest of your life, be it more or less, as your nature wills. Consider accordingly what it does will, and let nothing besides distract you; for experience has taught you in how many paths you have strayed and nowhere found the good life: not in logical arguments, not in riches, not in glory, not in self-indulgence, nowhere. Where then is it to be found?* In doing what man's nature requires. How then will he do this? If he hold fast doctrines upon which impulses and actions depend. What doctrines are these? They concern good and evil, how nothing is good for man which does not make him just, sober, brave, and free; nothing evil which does not produce effects the opposite of these.

2. On the occasion of each act, ask yourself: 'How is this related to me? Shall I repent of it? But a little while and I am dead and all things are taken away. What more do I require, if my present work is the work of an intelligent and social creature, subject to the same law as God?'

3.* Alexander, Julius Caesar, and Pompeius, what are they by comparison with Diogenes, Heraclitus, and Socrates? For these men saw reality and its causal and material aspects, and their ruling selves were self-determined; but as for the former, how much there was to provide for, and of how many things they were the servants.

4. Even if you break your heart, none the less they* will do just the same.

5. In the first place, be not troubled; for all things are according to Universal Nature, and in a little while you will be no one and nowhere, even as Hadrian and Augustus are no more. Next, looking earnestly at the question, perceive its essence, and reminding yourself that your duty is to be a good man, and what it is that man's nature demands, do that without swerving, and speak the thing that appears to you to be most just, provided only that it is with kindness and modesty, and without hypocrisy.

6. The work of Universal Nature is this: to transfer what is here to there, to make changes, to take up from here and to carry there. All things are alterations, but the assignments, too, are impartial: all things are familiar, but not so that we need dread some new experience.

7. Every natural thing is satisfied when it fares well, and a reasonable nature fares well when it gives its assent to nothing false or obscure in its imaginations, directs its impulses only to social ends, desires and avoids only what is in our power, and welcomes all that is assigned by Universal Nature. For it is a part of Universal Nature, just as the leaf's nature is part of the plant's, only in that case the leaf's nature is part of a Nature naturally without sense or reason and able to be hindered, whereas man's nature is part of a Nature which is unhindered and reasonable and just, inasmuch as it assigns to each, impartially and according to its worth, its share of times, substance, cause, activity, experience. Consider, however, not whether you will find one thing equal to another in everything, but whether the whole of this taken together is not equal to the whole of that other.

8.* You are not able to read; but you are able to restrain your arrogance, you are able to rise above pleasures and pains, you are able to be superior to fame, you are able not only not to be angry with the unfeeling and graceless, but to care for them besides.

9. Let no one any longer hear you finding fault with your life in a palace; nay, do not even hear yourself.

10. Regret is blame of oneself for having let something useful go by; but the good must be something useful and worth the attention of a really good man. Now no really good man would regret having let a pleasure go by: no pleasure, therefore, is either useful or good.

11. What is this by itself in its own constitution, what is its substance or substrate, what its causal element, what its function in the world and how long a time does it persist?

12. When you are called from sleep with difficulty,* revive the thought that to render social acts is according to your constitution and to human nature, but to sleep is what you share also with dumb animals. Now what to every creature is according to Nature is also more closely related to it, more part of its flesh and bone, yes, and also more agreeable.

13. Continually and, if possible, on the occasion of every imagination, test it by natural science, by psychology, by logic.*

14.* Whatever man you meet, say to yourself at once: 'what are the principles this man entertains about human goods and ills?' For if he has certain principles about pleasure and pain and the sources of these, about honour and dishonour, about death and life, it will not seem surprising or strange to me if he acts in certain ways, and I shall remember that he is obliged to act like this.

15. Remember that it is as absurd to be surprised that the world brings forth the fruits with which it teems as that the fig-tree should bear figs.* And it is absurd for the physician or the master of a ship to be surprised, if a patient is feverish or if a head wind gets up.

16.* Remember that to change your course and to follow someone who puts you right is not to be less free. For the change is your own action, proceeding according to your own impulse and decision, and indeed according to your mind.

17. If it is in your power to decide, why do you do it? But if in another's, whom do you find fault with? The atoms or the

gods? Either is madness. You must find fault with no one. If you are able, put him right; if you can't do this, at least put the thing itself right; but if you can't even do this, to what purpose still does fault-finding tend? For nothing should be done without a purpose.

18. What dies does not fall outside the Universe. If it remains here and changes here, it is also resolved here into the eternal constituents, which are elements of the Universe and of yourself. And the elements themselves change and make no grievance of it.

19. Each has come into being for a purpose—a horse, say, or a vine. Why are you surprised? So the Sun God will say: 'I came into being for a purpose', and the rest of the gods too. What then is the purpose of your coming to be? 'To please yourself?'* See whether the idea allows itself to be framed.

20. Nature has designed the ending of each thing, no less than its beginning and its continuance, like one who throws a ball up. What good is it to the ball to go up or harm to come down and even fall to the ground? What good to the bubble to be blown or harm to it to burst? The same is true of a candle.

21. Turn it inside out and see the sort of thing it is, what it is like when it grows old or falls sick or . . . [*gap in text*] Short-lived alike are praiser and the praised, he who remembers and he who is remembered. Moreover, they live in a mere corner of this region of the globe and even here all are not in accord, nor is even a man in accord with himself. The whole earth, too, is a mere point.*

22. Attend to the subject, the activity, the doctrine, or the meaning.

You deserve to suffer this; so you would rather become good tomorrow than be good today.

23. Am I doing something? I relate the act to beneficence to men. Does an accident befall me? I accept it, relating it to the gods and to the source of all things, from which all that comes to pass depends by a common thread.

24.* As your bath appears to your senses—soap, sweat, dirt, greasy water, all disgusting—so is every piece of life and every object.

25.* Lucilla laid Verus in the grave, Lucilla followed; Secunda buried Maximus, Secunda next; Epitynchanus buried Diotimus, Epitynchanus next; Antoninus Faustina, Antoninus next. The same story over again. Celer Hadrian, Celer came next. Where now are those acute minds, those who unveiled the future, those who were swollen with pride? acute minds like Charax and Demetrius and Eudaemon and others of their kind. All creatures of a day, dead long since; some remembered not even for a little while, some turned to fable, and some even now fading out of fable. Keep these facts in mind, that your own frame is bound either to be scattered into atoms or your spirit to be extinguished or to change its place and be stationed somewhere else.

26. A man's joy is to do what is proper to man, and man's proper work is kindness to his fellow man, disdain of the movements of the senses, to discern plausible imaginations, to meditate on Universal Nature and the work of her hands.

27. There are three relations: one to your environment, one to the divine cause from which all things come to pass for all, one to those who live at the same time with you.

28. Pain is an evil, either to the body, in which case let the body say that it is so, or to the soul. But it is in the soul's power to preserve its own quiet and calm,* and not to judge pain to be an evil; for every judgement, impulse, desire, or aversion is within, and nothing evil makes its way up to this.

29. Wipe out impressions by continually saying to yourself: it is in my power now not to allow any wickedness to be in this soul of mine, any appetite or disturbance at all, but seeing what is the character of them all I employ each according to its worth. Remember this power as Nature requires.

30.* Speak both in the senate and to every man of whatever

rank with propriety, without affectation. Use words that ring
true.

31. The court of Augustus, his wife, daughter, grandsons,
stepsons, sister, Agrippa, his kinsmen, familiar friends, Areios,*
Maecenas,* doctors, sacrificial ministers—a whole court dead.
Next pass on to other courts—death not of a single individual,
but of a family, like the children of Pompeius. Then the familiar
inscription upon tombs: THE LAST OF HIS LINE. Calculate all
the anxiety of those who preceded them in order to leave behind
an heir, and then it was ordained that one should be the last; here
again a whole family dead.

32. You must plan your life, one action at a time, and be content if each acquires its own end as best it can; and that it should
acquire its end, no one at all can prevent you. 'But some external
obstacle will be in the way.' None to prevent action with justice,
temperance, and due reflection. 'But possibly some other activity
will be hindered.' Still, by meeting the actual obstacle with
resignation and good-temperedly altering your course to what is
granted you, a new action is at once substituted, which will fit
into the plan of which we are speaking.

33. Accept without pride, relinquish without a struggle.

34. If you have ever seen a dismembered hand or foot or a
head cut off,* lying somewhere apart from the rest of the trunk,
you have an image of what a man makes of himself, so far as in
him lies, when he refuses to associate his will with what happens
and cuts himself off or when he does some unneighbourly act.
You have somehow made yourself an outcast from the unity
which is according to Nature; for you came into the world as a
part and now you have cut yourself off. Yet here there is this admirable provision that it is in your power to make yourself once
more part of the unity—God has permitted this to no other part,
to come together again, once it has been severed and cut off. But
consider the kindness with which he has honoured man. He has
put it in his power, to begin with, not to be broken off from the
Whole, and then, if he has been broken off, to come back again

once more and to grow together and to recover his portion as a part.

35. As each reasonable creature receives the rest of his abilities from the Nature of the Whole, so have we received this ability, too, from her. Just as she converts every obstacle and resistance, puts it into its place in the order of necessity and makes it a part of herself, so, too, the reasonable creature can make every obstacle material for himself and employ it for whatever kind of purpose he has set out upon.

36. Do not allow the imagination of the whole of your life to confuse you, do not dwell upon all the manifold troubles which have come to pass and will come to pass, but ask yourself in regard to every present piece of work: what is there here that can't be borne and can't be endured? You will be ashamed to make the confession. Then remind yourself that it is not the future or the past that weighs heavy upon you, but always the present, and that this gradually grows less, if only you isolate it and reprove your understanding, if that is not strong enough to hold out against it, thus taken by itself.

37. Is Panthea* or Pergamos* still sitting by the funeral bier of Verus; Chabrias or Diotimus* by Hadrian's bier? Absurd! And if they were still sitting there, would the dead perceive it? And if they did perceive it, would it give them pleasure? And, if it gave them pleasure, would the mourners live for ever? Were not they too fated first to become old men and women, and then to die? And when they were dead, what would those they mourned do afterwards? This is all a smell of corruption and blood, and dust in a winding sheet.

38. If you have a sharp sight; 'see', says he,* 'and judge, by the wisest judgements you have.'

39. In the constitution of a reasonable creature I see no virtue able to oppose justice: but I see one able to oppose pleasure, self-control.

40. If you cancel your judgement about what seems to pain you, you yourself stand firm on surest ground. 'What is self?'

'Reason.' 'But I am not reason.' 'Granted; then do not let reason itself trouble itself, but if some other part of you is harmed, let it form its own judgement about itself.'

41. An obstacle to sense perception is injurious to animal nature; an obstacle to impulse is equally injurious to animal nature. (And something else may similarly be an obstacle and injurious to the constitution of a plant.) Thus then an obstacle to reason is injurious to a reasoning nature. Transfer, therefore, all these considerations to yourself. Perhaps pain and pleasure are affecting you. Sense affection must look to it. Did an obstacle oppose your impulse? If you started out to satisfy it without mental reservation, the obstacle is at once injurious to you as a reasonable being; but if you experience the general lot, you are not yet hurt or hindered. The properties of the mind, you know, no one else is wont to hinder, for neither fire nor steel nor despot nor abuse affect it one whit, when it has become 'a sphere rounded and at rest'.*

42. I do not deserve to give myself pain, for I never deliberately gave another pain.

43. One thing gives joy to one man, another to another; it is my joy if I keep my governing self intact, not turning my back on any human being nor on anything that befalls men, but seeing everything with kind eyes, welcoming and employing each occasion according to its merits.

44. See that you bestow this present time upon yourself. Those who rather run after fame in the future leave out of account that men hereafter will be just such others as these whom they find hard to bear, and those men, too, will be liable to death. What, after all, is it to you if men hereafter resound your name with such and such voices or have such and such a judgement about you?

45. 'Take me up and cast me where you please.' For there I shall keep the divinity within me propitious; satisfied, that is, if it should behave and act consistently with its own constitution.
Is this a sufficient reason why my soul should be in evil case,

should lower itself, be humbled, craving, fettered, fluttering? What will you discover to be a sufficient reason for that?

46. Nothing can happen to any human being which is not an incident appropriate to man, nor to an ox which is not appropriate to oxen, nor to a vine which is not appropriate to vines, nor to a stone which is not peculiar to a stone. If then that happens to each which is both customary and natural, why should you be discontented with your lot? For the Universal Nature did not bring to you what you could not bear.

47. If you suffer pain because of some external cause, what troubles you is not the thing but your decision about it, and this it is in your power to wipe out at once. But if what pains you is something in your own disposition, who prevents you from correcting your judgement? And similarly, if you are pained because you fail in some particular action which you imagine to be sound, why not continue to act rather than to feel pain? 'But something too strong for you opposes itself.' Then do not be pained, for the reason why the act is not done does not rest with you. 'Well, but if this be left undone, life is not worth living.' Depart then from life* in a spirit of good will, even as he dies who achieves his end, contented, too, with what opposes you.

48. Remember that the governing self becomes invincible* when it withdraws into itself and is satisfied with itself, doing nothing which it does not will to do, even if its opposition is unreasonable. How much more then when it decides both with reason and circumspection about a given case? On this account the understanding free from passions is a citadel of refuge;* for man has nothing stronger into which to retreat and be thereafter inexpugnable. He then who has not seen this is uninstructed; he who has seen it and does not retreat is unfortunate.

49. Do not say more to yourself than the first impressions report. You have been told that some one speaks evil of you. This is what you have been told; you have not been told that you are injured. I see that the little child is ill; this is what I see, but that he is in danger I do not see. In this way then abide always by

the first impressions and add nothing of your own from within, and that's an end of it; or rather one thought you may add, as one who is acquainted with every change and chance of the world.

50. The cucumber is bitter? Put it down. There are brambles in the path? Step to one side. That is enough, without also asking: 'Why did these things come into the world at all?' Because the student of Nature will ridicule the question, exactly as a carpenter or cobbler would laugh at you if you found fault because you see shavings and clippings* from their work in their shops. Still, they do have a place to throw rubbish into, whereas Universal Nature has nothing outside himself, and yet the astonishing thing in *her* way of working is that, having fixed her own limits, she is ever changing into herself everything within those limits that looks as though it were going bad and getting old and useless, and out of these very things creating again others that are young, in order that she may need no substance from outside nor require any place to throw away what begins to decay. Thus she is satisfied with her own room, her own material and her own way of working.

51. Be not a sluggard in action nor confused in conversation nor wandering in imagination. Briefly, neither contract into yourself nor boil over in spirit nor in your mode of life leave no room for leisure.

'They kill you, cut you in pieces, pursue you with curses.'* What has this to do with your understanding abiding pure, sane, temperate, and just? As if a man should stand by a sweet and crystal spring* of water and curse it, but it never ceases bubbling up in water fresh to drink, and if he throw in mud or dung, it will quickly break it up and wash it away and will in no way be discoloured. How then shall you possess an overflowing fountain, not a mere cistern? If you guard yourself every hour unto freedom, contentedly, too, simply and reverently.

52*. He who does not know that the Universe exists, does not know where he is. He who does not know the purpose of the Universe, does not know who he is nor what the Universe is. He who fails in any one of these respects could not even declare the purpose of his own birth. What then do you imagine him to be, who shuns or pursues the praises of men who applaud, and yet do not know either where they are or who they are?

53. Do you wish to be praised by a man who curses himself three times every hour? Do you wish to please a man who doesn't please himself? Does a man please himself who repents of nearly everything that he does?

54. No longer merely breathe with the atmosphere that surrounds you, but now think also with the mind that surrounds all things. For the power of mind is as much poured out everywhere and distributed for him who is willing to absorb it, as the power of atmosphere for him who is able to respire it.

55. In general evil does no injury to the Universe, and particular evil does no injury to a neighbour, but only injures him to whom it is permitted to be delivered from it as soon as ever he himself determines.

56. To my will the will of a neighbour is as indifferent as his vital spirit and his flesh. For even though we were brought into the world more than anything else for the sake of one another, still each of our governing selves has its own sovereign right; for otherwise the evil of my neighbour would surely be evil of mine, and that was not God's good pleasure, in order that my unhappiness might not depend on someone other than myself.

57. The sun appears to be poured down and indeed is poured in every direction but not poured out. For this pouring is extension, and so its beams are called rays from their being extended.* Now you may see what kind of thing a ray is by observing the sun's light streaming through a chink into a darkened room. For it is stretched in a straight line, and rests so to speak upon any solid body that meets it and cuts off the flow of air beyond. It rests there and does not glide off or fall. The pouring and diffusion of the understanding then should be similar, in no way a pouring out, but an extension, and it should not rest forcibly or violently on obstacles that meet it nor yet fall down, but stand

still and illuminate the object that receives it; for that which does not reflect it will rob itself of the light.

58. He who fears death fears either total loss of consciousness or a change of consciousness. Now if you should no longer possess consciousness, you will no longer be aware of any evil; alternatively, if you possess an altered consciousness, you will be an altered creature and will not cease from living.

59. Men have come into the world for the sake of one another. Either instruct them then or bear with them.

60. An arrow's path and the mind's path are different. Nevertheless, both when it is on its guard and when it revolves round a subject of inquiry, the path of mind is none the less direct and upon its object.

61. Enter into the governing self of every man and permit every other man to enter into your own.

BOOK IX

1. Whosoever does injustice commits sin; for Universal Nature having made reasonable creatures for the sake of one another, to benefit each other according to desert but in no wise to do injury, manifestly he who transgresses her will sins against the most venerable of the gods, because Universal Nature is a nature of what is, and what is is related to all that exists.

And further, he who lies sins in regard to the same divine being, and she is named Truth and is the first cause of all truths. Now he who lies voluntarily commits sin in so far as by deceit he does injustice, and he who lies involuntarily sins, in so far as he is discordant with Universal Nature and creates disorder by fighting against the natural order of the Universe; for he who is carried of himself counter to truth does so fight, since he had before received from Nature aptitudes by neglecting which he is now not able to distinguish falsehood from truth.

Moreover, he who runs after pleasures as goods and away from pains as evils commits sin; for being such a man he must necessarily often blame Universal Nature for distributing to bad and good contrary to their desert, because the bad are often employed in pleasures and acquire what may produce these, while the good are involved in pain and in what may produce this.

And further, he who fears pains will sometimes fear what is to come to pass in the Universe, and this is at once sinful, while he who pursues pleasures will not abstain from doing injustice, and this is plainly sinful. But those who wish to follow Nature, being like-minded with her, must be indifferent towards the things to which she is indifferent, for she would not create both were she not indifferent towards both. Whosoever, therefore, is not himself indifferent to pain and pleasure, death and life, honour and dishonour, which Universal Nature employs indifferently, plainly commits sin.

And by 'Universal Nature employing these indifferently', I mean that in the natural order they happen indifferently to what comes to pass and follows upon an original impulse of Providence, whereby from an original cause it had an impulse to this world order, having conceived certain principles of what should come to be, and appointed powers generative of substances and changes and successions of the like kind.

2. A wiser man's part had been to go away from men without tasting falsehood, hypocrisy, luxury, and pride; a second-best course is to breathe your last filled at least with distaste for these things. Or is it your choice to sit down with wickedness and does not your experience even yet persuade you to flee from the plague?* For corruption of understanding is much more a plague than such a distemper and change of this environing atmosphere; for this is a plague to animals,* as animate beings, that is a plague to men, as human beings.

3. Disdain not death, but be well satisfied with it, because this, too, is one of the things which Nature wills. For as are adolescence and old age, growth and maturity, development of teeth and beard and grey hair, begetting, conception, and childbearing and the rest of the natural functions which life's seasons bring, such also is actual dissolution. This, therefore, is like a man of trained reason, not to be rash or violent or disdainful in the face of death, but to wait for it as one of the natural functions; and, as you now wait for the unborn child to come forth from your wife's womb,* so expect the hour in which your soul will drop from this shell.

And if you would have an everyday rule to touch your heart, it will make you most contented with death to dwell upon the objects from which you are about to be parted and the kind of characters* with whom your soul will be no longer contaminated. For you should in no wise be offended by them, but rather both care for them and bear them gently, yet still remember that your deliverance will not be from men like-minded* with yourself. This alone, if anything could, might draw you back and detain you in life, were it granted you to live with those who had adopted the same doctrines; but, as it is, you see how great is the burden in the discord of life lived with them, so that you say: 'Come swiftly, death, for fear I, too, forget myself.'

4. Whosoever does wrong, wrongs himself; whosoever does injustice, does it to himself, making himself evil.

5. Often he who omits an act does injustice, not only he who commits an act.

6. Sufficient are the present judgement that grasps its object, the present social act, the present disposition well satisfied with all that comes to pass from a cause outside the self.

7. Wipe out imagination: check impulse: quench desire: keep the governing self in its own control.

8. One vital spirit is distributed in irrational creatures: one mind spirit is divided in rational creatures; just as one element earth is in all earthy things and we see by one light and breathe one atmosphere, all that have sight and vital spirit.

9. All that partake in something common to them hasten towards what is of the same kind. The earthy all tends to earth, the watery all flows together, and the nature of air is similar so that they even need things to hold them apart by compulsion. Fire rises because of the elemental fire, but is so ready to combine in combustion with all fire here below that every material that is a little too dry is easily ignited, because what hinders ignition is mixed in it in too small proportions. Therefore also, all that partakes of a common mind similarly, or even more swiftly, hastens to what is akin; for in proportion as it is superior to the rest, so is it more ready to mix and be blended with its own kind.

At any rate there were found from the first* among irrational creatures, hives, and flocks, care for nestlings, and what resembles love; for already there were vital spirits there, and in the higher part the tendency to union was found raised in degree, as it was not in plants or minerals or trees. Among reasonable creatures, constitutions, friendships, households, and gatherings were found, conventions too and armistices in war. Among the yet higher, even among beings in a sense separated, there subsisted a unity such as obtains among the stars. Thus progress towards the higher was able to produce a sympathy even in what are separated.

Notice then what occurs now; only intelligent creatures have now forgotten that zeal and inclination to each other, and here only you do not see concurrence. Yet even so, they are overtaken in their flight, for nature is too strong for them.* Watch and you will observe what I mean; certainly one would more quickly discover something earthy not attaching itself to the earthy than man entirely cut off from man.

10. Man, God, and the Universe alike bear fruit, each in the appropriate season, but if custom has come to apply the word strictly of the vine and similar fruits, no matter. Reason, too, has its fruit, for the Whole and for itself, and from reason other results similar to itself come to pass.

11. If you can, change him by teaching, but if you cannot, remember that kindness was given you for this. The gods, too, are kind* to such men and even co-operate with them to some objects, to health, to wealth, to reputation, so good are they to men; and you may be so too; or say, who is there to prevent you?

12. Labour, not like one who is unfortunate, nor wishing to be pitied or admired: rather have only one wish: to bestir yourself or to keep quiet as the reason of the City requires.

13. Today I escaped all circumstance, or rather I cast out all circumstance, for it was not outside me, but within, in my judgements.

14. All things are the same: familiar in experience, transient in time, sordid in their material; all now such as in the days of those whom we have buried.

15.* Things stand outside our doors, themselves by themselves, neither knowing nor reporting anything about themselves. What then does report about them? The governing self.

16. Not in feeling but in action is the good and ill of the reasonable social creature; even as his excellence and his failings are not in feeling but in action.

17. To the stone that is thrown up it is no ill to be carried down nor good to be carried upwards.

18. Penetrate within, into their governing selves, and you will see what critics you fear, and what poor critics they are of themselves.

19. All things are in change, and you yourself in continuous alteration and in a sense destruction. So, too, is the Universe as a whole.

20.* Another's wrong act you must leave where it is.

21.* The ceasing of action, impulse, judgement is a pause and a kind of death, not any evil. Now pass to the ages of your life, boyhood for instance, youth, manhood, old age; for each change of these was a death; was it anything to be afraid of? Pass now to your manner of life under your grandfather, then under your mother, then under your (adoptive) father, and when you discover many another destruction, change, and ending, ask yourself: 'Was it anything to be afraid of?' So then even the ceasing, pause, and change of your whole life is not.

22. Make haste to your own governing self, to that of the Whole, and that of this man. To your own, to make it a righteous mind; to that of the whole, to remind yourself what it is of which you are a part; to this man's, that you may observe whether it is ignorance or design,* and may reflect at the same time that his self is of one kind with your own.

23. As you are yourself a complement of a social system, so let every act of yours be complementary of a social living principle. Every act of yours, therefore, which is not referred directly or remotely to the social end sunders your life, does not allow it to be a unity, and is a partisan act, like a man in a republic who for his own part sunders himself from the harmony of his fellows.

24. Children's fits of temper and dolls and 'spirits carrying dead bodies',* so that the story of the visit to the abode of Death* strikes one more vividly.

25. Penetrate to the individuality of the cause and separating it from the matter, look into it; next isolate the time which at longest this individuality can by its nature subsist.

26. You endure a myriad troubles because you are not content with your governing self doing the kind of things it was formed to do. But enough.

27. When another blames or hates you or men express such sentiments, go to their inward selves, pass in and see what kind of men they are. You will see that you ought not to torment yourself in order that they may hold some opinion about you. You must, however, be well disposed to them; for in the natural order they are friends, and moreover the gods help them in a variety of ways, by dreams, by prophecy;* to get, however, the objects about which they are concerned.

28. The rotations of the Universe are the same, up and down, from age to age.

Now either the mind of the Whole has an impulse to each individual; and if that is so, welcome what it initiates; or else it had an impulse once for all and what follows is consequential upon that; and why are you anxious? And whether the Whole be God, all is well—or whether it be Chance, somehow molecules or atoms, be not yourself then ruled by Chance.

29. In a moment earth will cover us all, then earth, too, will change and what ensues will change to eternity and that again to eternity. A man who thinks of the continuous waves of change and alteration, and the swift passage of all mortal things, will hold them in disdain.

29. The matter of the Whole is a torrent; it carries all in its stream. What then, man, is your part? Act as Nature this moment requires; set about it, if it is granted you, and don't look round to see whether anyone will know. Don't hope for Plato's Utopia,* but be content to make a very small step forward and reflect that the result even of this is no trifle. How cheap are these mere men with their policies* and their philosophic practice, as they suppose; they are full of drivel.* For who will

change men's convictions? And without a change of conviction
what else is there save a bondage of men who groan and pretend
to obey? Go to now and talk to me of Alexander, Philip, and
Demetrius of Phalerum.* If they saw what Universal Nature
willed and went to school to her, I will follow: but if they were
actors on the world's stage,* no one has condemned me to imitate
them. The work of Philosophy is simplicity and self-respect; lead
me not away to vainglory.

30.* 'Look from above' at the spectacle of myriad herds,
myriad rites, and manifold journeying in storm and calm; diver-
sities of creatures who are being born, coming together, passing
away. Ponder, too, the life led by others long ago, the life that
will be led after you, the life being led in uncivilized races; how
many do not even know your name, how many will very soon
forget it and how many who praise you perhaps now will very
soon blame you; and that neither memorial nor fame nor
anything else at all is worth a thought.

31. Calm, in respect of what comes to pass from a cause outside you; justice, in acts done in accord with a cause from
yourself: that is to say, impulse and act terminating simply in
neighbourly conduct, because for you this is according to
Nature.

32. You have the power to strip off many superfluities which
trouble you and are wholly in your own judgement; and you will
make a large room at once for yourself by embracing in your
thought the whole Universe,* grasping ever-continuing Time
and pondering the rapid change in the parts of each object, how
brief the interval from birth to dissolution, and the time before
birth a yawning gulf even as the period after dissolution equally
boundless.

33. All that your eyes behold will very quickly pass away, and
those who saw it passing will themselves also pass away very
quickly; and he who dies in extreme age will be made equal in
years with the infant who meets an untimely end.

34. What governing selves are theirs, what mean ends have

they pursued, for what mean reasons do they give love and esteem! Accustom yourself to look at their souls in nakedness.* When they fancy that their blame hurts or their praise profits, how great their vanity.

35. Loss is nothing else but change. In this Universal Nature rejoices and by her all things come to pass well. From eternity they came to pass in like fashion and will be to everlasting in other similar shapes. Why then do you say 'all things ever came to pass badly and that all will ever be bad'? So no power it seems was ever found in so many gods to remedy this,* but the world is condemned to be straitened in uninterrupted evils?

36.* The rottenness of the matter which underlies everything. Water, dust, bones, stench. Again: marble, an incrustation of earth; gold and silver, sediments; your dress, the hair of animals; the purple dye, blood, and so all the rest. What is of the nature of breath too is similar and changing from this to that.

37. Enough of this wretched way of life, of complaining and mimicry. Why are you troubled, what novelty is there in this, what takes you out of yourself? The formal side of things? Look it in the face. The material side then? Face that. Besides these there is nothing, except even now at this late hour to become simpler and better in your relation to the gods. To acquaint yourself with these things for a hundred years or for three is the same.

38. If he did wrong, the harm is with him; but perhaps he did not.

39. Either all comes to pass from one fountain of mind, as in a single organic body, and the part must not find fault with what is for the good of the whole; or else there are atoms,* nothing but a mechanical mixture and dispersal. Why then be troubled? Say to your governing self: 'are you dead, gone to corruption. turned into a beast, are you acting a part, running with the herd, feeding with it?'

40. The gods are either powerless or powerful. If then they are powerless, why do you pray? But if they are powerful, why not

rather pray them for the gift to fear none of these things, to desire none of them, to sorrow for none of them, rather than that any one of them should be present or absent? For surely if they can co-operate with man, they can co-operate to these ends. But perhaps you will say: 'The gods put these things in my power.'* Were it not better then to use what is in your power with a free spirit rather than to be concerned for what is not in your power with a servile and abject spirit? Besides, who told you that the gods do not co-operate even in respect to what is in our power?* Begin at least to pray about these things and you will see. That man prays: 'How may I know that woman'; do *you* pray: 'How may I not desire to know her.' Another prays: 'How may I get rid of him'; do *you* pray: 'How may I not want to be rid of him.' Another: 'How may I not lose my little child'; do *you* pray: 'How may I not be afraid to lose him.' Turn your prayers round in this way generally and see what is the result.

41. Epicurus says:* 'In illness* my conversation was not about the sufferings of my body, nor used I', he says, 'to talk to my visitors about such matters, but I continued to debate leading principles of science and to keep only to this, how the understanding while conscious of such changes in the mere flesh is yet undisturbed and preserves its own proper good. I did not even', he goes on, 'permit the medical men to give themselves airs as though they were doing some great thing, but my life passed on happily and brightly.' Do the same then as he did, in sickness if you are sick and in any other circumstance, for it is common to every school not to desert Philosophy in any at all of the accidents of life and not to gossip with the ignorant and unlearned. Be intent only on what is now being done and on the instrument you use to do it.

42*. Whenever you are offended by a man's shamelessness, ask yourself immediately: 'Is it possible then for the shameless not to be in the world?' It is not; do not then ask for the impossible;* for he, too, is one of the shameless who must exist in the world. And have the same ready also for the rogue, the traitor, and every kind of wrongdoer; for directly you remind yourself that the class of such persons cannot but be, you will be gentler to them as individuals. Another useful thing is to call to mind immediately what virtue Nature gave man to meet this wrong, for she gave as an antidote against the unfeeling, mildness, against another, some other faculty, and generally speaking it is in your power to convert the man who has gone astray, for every man who does wrong is going wrong from the goal set before him and has gone astray. And what harm have you suffered? For you will find that none of those with whom you are angry has done the kind of thing by which your understanding was likely to become worse and it is there that your ills and harms have their entire existence.

How is it an evil or strange event that the uninstructed does what uninstructed men do? See whether you should not rather find fault with yourself for not expecting that he would do this wrong; for you had aptitudes from reason to enable you to argue that in all probability this man will do this wrong, and yet you forgot and are surprised that he did wrong.

But, most important of all, turn inward to your own self, whenever you blame the traitor or the ungrateful, for the fault is plainly yours, whether you trusted a man with such a disposition to keep faith or whether, when you bestowed a favour,* you did not give it unreservedly or so that you received the whole fruit from your act itself then and there. For when you have done good, what more, oh man, do you wish? Is it not enough that what you did was in agreement with your nature and do you seek a recompense for this? As if the eye asked a return for seeing or the feet for walking;* for just as these were made for this which they effect according to their proper constitution, and so get what is theirs, even thus man is made by Nature to be benevolent, and whenever he contributes to the common stock by benevolence or otherwise, he has done what he was constituted for, and gets what is his own.

BOOK X

1. Wilt thou one day, my soul, be good, simple, single, naked, plainer to see than the body surrounding thee? Wilt thou one day taste a loving and devoted disposition? Wilt thou one day be filled and without want, craving nothing and desiring nothing, animate or inanimate, for indulgence in pleasures; not time wherein longer to indulge thyself, nor happy situation of place or room or breezes nor harmony of men? Wilt thou rather be satisfied with present circumstance and pleased with all the present, and convince thyself that all is present for thee from the gods and all is well for thee and will be well whatsoever is dear to them to give and whatsoever they purpose to bestow for the sustenance of the perfect living creature, the good and just and beautiful, which begets, sustains, includes, and embraces all things that are being resolved into the generation of others like themselves? Wilt thou one day be such as to dwell in the society of gods and men so as neither to find fault at all with them nor to be condemned by them?

2. Observe what your nature requires in so far as you are governed by mere physical nature; then do that and accept that, if only your nature as part of the animal world will not be rendered worse. Next you are to observe what your nature as part of the animal world requires and to take it all, if only your nature as a reasonable being will not be rendered worse. But what is reasonable is consequently also social. Make use then of these rules and do not be troubled about anything besides.

3. Every event happens in such a way that your nature can either support it or cannot. If then it happens so that your nature can support it, do not complain but support it as it is your nature to do; but if so that your nature cannot support it, do not complain, for it will destroy you quickly. Remember, however, that your nature can support everything which it is in the power of

your own judgement to make tolerable and endurable by representing to yourself that to do this is to your advantage or is your duty.

4. If he goes wrong, instruct him kindly and point out what is being overlooked; if you fail, blame yourself or, better, not even yourself.

5. Whatever befalls you was prepared for you beforehand from eternity and the thread of causes was spinning from everlasting both your existence and this which befalls you.

6. Whether there are Atoms* or Nature, the first postulate must be: 'I am part of the Whole which is governed by Nature'; the second: 'I am allied in some way to the parts that are of the same kind with me.' For if I remember these postulates, I shall, in so far as I am a part, not be disaffected to anything assigned by the Whole; for nothing which benefits the Whole is injurious to the part,* since the Whole contains nothing which does not benefit itself, and while all natural existences have this common attribute, the nature of the Universe has this further attribute that no external cause can compel it to generate anything injurious to itself.

By remembering, therefore, that I am a part of a Whole so characterized, I shall be well-affected to all that results from it, and inasmuch as I am allied in some way to the parts of the same kind as myself, I will do no unsocial act, rather I will study the good of my kind and direct every impulse to the common benefit and divert it from what opposes that benefit. Now when things are being accomplished in this way, life must needs flow smoothly, just as you would see that a citizen's life is smooth as he progresses by acts which benefit his fellow citizens and welcomes whatever his city assigns.

7. The parts of the Whole, all which the Universe naturally includes, must necessarily perish, a word which is to be interpreted to denote change. Now if this were naturally evil as well as necessary for the parts, the Whole would not continue to be in a right condition while its parts were tending to change and

had been put together specifically with a view to perishing. (For whether did* Nature herself undertake to injure the parts of herself and to create them with a tendency to evil, and bound by necessity to fall into evil, or did such things come to pass without her knowledge? Neither view is credible.)

But now suppose one dispensed with Nature and expounded facts by way of 'natural law'; how absurd it is in one breath to assert that the parts of the Whole change by natural law, and in the same moment to be surprised or indignant as though at an occurrence in violation of natural law, particularly when the dissolution of each is taking place into the elements out of which each is composed. For this dissolution is either a dissipation of the atoms out of which they were compounded or else a turning of the solid into its earthy and of the vital spirit into its airy part, so that these too are caught up into the Reason of the Whole, whether the Whole returns periodically* to fire or is renewed by eternal exchanges.

And do not imagine this solid body and this vital spirit to be that of its original entry into existence, for all this it took in only yesterday or the day before, an influx from foodstuffs and the atmosphere which is respired; what is changing then is what it took in, not what its mother brought into the world. And even suppose that what thus is changing binds you intimately to the individual self, that is in fact nothing, I think, to affect my present argument.

8. After giving yourself these titles: good, self-respecting, true, sane, conforming, high-minded, take care not to get others in their place; and, if you do lose these titles, be quick to return to them. Remember, further, that 'sanity' was intended to denote apprehensive attention to individual objects and the reverse of negligence; 'conformity' glad acceptance of the assignments of Universal Nature; and 'high-mindedness' elevation of the thinking part above the smooth or interrupted movement of the flesh, above petty reputation and death and all indifferent things.

Therefore, if you continue to preserve yourself in these titles, not aspiring to be called them by others, you will be a changed man and will enter upon a changed life.* For still to be such as you have been up to the present, to be torn and polluted in such a way of life, is to be utterly brutalized, to cling to mere life like half-devoured combatants in the arena,* a mass of wounds and dusty blood, yet imploring to be kept alive until the morrow, only to be exposed in that state to the same teeth and claws.

Adventure yourself then upon these few titles, and if you are able to abide in them, abide like a man translated to Islands of the Blest; but if you perceive that you are falling away and losing control, go bravely away into some corner, there to recover control, or even depart altogether from life,* not angrily, but simply* and freely and with self-respect, having done at least this one thing in life, to have made your exit thus.

To remember the titles, however, it will be a great help to you to remember the gods, and that they at least do not wish to be the objects of servility, but for all rational beings to be made into their likeness,* and that the fig-tree should be what does the work of a fig-tree, the dog of a dog, the bee of a bee, and man the work of a man.

9. Play-acting, warfare, excitement, lethargy—in fact slavery! Every day those sacred doctrines of yours, whichever of them you imagine and admit without scientific investigation, will be obliterated, whereas you should look at every object and do every act so that, at one and the same time, circumstance is accomplished and theory exercised, and the confidence which comes from a scientific knowledge of each experience is preserved, unnoticed, not concealed. For when will you take your indulgence in simplicity, when in dignity, when in the knowledge of what each object is in essence, what station it holds in the world, how long it naturally persists, of what it is compounded, to whom it can belong, who can give it and who take it away?

10. A spider is proud when he traps a fly, a man when he snares a leveret, another when he nets a sprat, another boars, another bears, another Sarmatian prisoners.* If you test their sentiments, are they not bandits?

11. Acquire a methodical insight into the way all things change, one into another; attend continually to this part of

Nature and exercise yourself in it, for nothing is so likely to promote an elevation of mind. He has put off the body and, reflecting that he will be bound almost at once to leave all these things behind and to depart from men, he has devoted his whole self to justice in what is being accomplished by himself, and to Universal Nature in what comes to pass otherwise. And he spends no thought about what someone may say or think about him or do against him, but is contented with these two things, if he is himself acting justly in what is done in the present, and if he embraces what is assigned to him in the present; and he has put away every preoccupation and enthusiasm, and has no other will than to pursue a straight path according to the law and, pursuing it, to follow in God's train.

12. What need have you of a hint or suggestion, when it is possible to see what ought to be done and, if you are conscious of that, kindly to proceed on this path without turning back; but if you are not conscious of it, to suspend judgement and use the best men to advise you; or if some further points bar this advice, to go forward according to your present opportunities cautiously, holding fast to what seems to be just? For it is best to achieve justice, since, as you see, failure is to fail in this. The man who in everything follows the rule of Reason is at once master of his time and quick to act, at once cheerful in expression and composed.

13. Ask yourself directly you awake from sleep: will it be of any moment to you, if just and right acts are blamed by another? No, it will not. Have you forgotten what these who plume themselves upon praise or censure of others are like at bed and board, the sort of things they do and avoid or pursue, how they steal and plunder, not with hands and feet, but with the most precious part of themselves, in which, whenever it determines, faith, self-respect, truth, law, a good divinity come into being?

14. To Nature, who bestows all things and takes them away, the man who has learnt his lesson and respects himself says:'Give what is thy good pleasure, take back what is thy good pleasure'; and this he says not boasting himself but only listening to her voice and being of one mind with her.

15. Small is this balance of life left to you. Live as on a height; for here or there matters nothing, if everywhere one lives in the Universe, as in a city.* Let men see, let them study a true man, a man who lives in accord with Nature. If they cannot bear him, let them kill him, for it were better so than for him to live on those terms.

16. Don't any more discuss at large what the good man is like, but be good.

17. Let your imagination dwell continually upon the whole of Time and the whole of Substance, and realize that their several parts are, by comparison with Substance, a fig-seed; by comparison with Time, the turn of a gimlet.

18. Dwell upon everything that exists and reflect that it is already in process of dissolution and coming into being by change and a kind of decay or dispersion, or in what way it is born to die, in a manner of speaking.

19. What creatures they are; they eat, sleep, copulate, relieve nature, and so on; then what are they like as rulers, imperious or angry and fault-finding to excess; yet but yesterday how many masters were they slaving for and to what purpose, and to-morrow they will be in a like condition.

20. Each man's benefit is what Universal Nature brings to each, and it is his benefit precisely at the time she brings it.

21. 'Earth loves the rain':* 'the glorious ether loves to fall in rain'. The Universe, too, loves to create what is to be. Therefore I say to the Universe: 'Your love is mine.' Is not that also the meaning of the phrase: 'This loves to happen'?

22. Either you go on living in the world and are familiar with it by now, or you go out, and that by your own will, or else you die and your service* is accomplished. There is nothing beside these three: therefore be of good courage.

23. Always realize vividly the saying that one place of retreat is like any other, and how everything in the place you are in is

the same as it would be on the top of a hill or by the sea or wherever you choose. You will find exactly what Plato says:* 'building round himself a fold on a hill and milking his bleating flocks'.

24. What is my governing self to me, and what sort of thing am I making it now, and for what purpose am I employing it now? Is it void of reason? Is it severed and torn asunder from society? Is it so melted into and blended with the flesh that it conforms to its movements?

25. He who runs away from his master is a fugitive slave. But law is a master and therefore the transgressor of law is a fugitive slave. In the same way, also, he who gives way to sorrow or anger or fear, wishes that something had not been or were not now, or should not be hereafter, of what is appointed by that which ordains all things; and that is law, laying down for every man what falls to his lot. He, therefore, who yields to fear or pain or anger is a fugitive slave.

26.* A man drops seed into a womb and goes his way and thereupon another causal principle takes it, labours upon it and completes a new-born babe. What a marvellous result of that small beginning. Next the babe passes food through the gullet and thereupon another causal principle takes it and creates sensation and impulse; in a word, life and strength and other results, how many and how marvellous. Contemplate, therefore, in thought what comes to pass in such a hidden way, and see the power, as we see the force which makes things gravitate or tend upwards, not with the eyes, but none the less clearly.

27. Reflect continually how all things came to pass in days gone by as they do today, and reflect that so they will hereafter; and put before your eyes whole dramas and scenes* of the same kind, which you have known in your own experience or from earlier history, the whole court of Hadrian, for instance, or of Antoninus; of Philip,* Alexander, and Croesus;* for those were all like these; the actors only were different.

28. Picture to yourself every man who gives way to pain or

discontent at any thing at all as like a pig being sacrificed, kicking and squealing. Such also is the man who groans on his bed, alone and in silence. Think of the chain we are bound by, and that to the rational creature only is it given to obey circumstances of his own will, while mere obedience is necessary for all.*

29. At the time of each separate act, stop and ask yourself whether death is to be feared because you are deprived of this.

30. When you run against someone's wrong behaviour, go on at once to reflect what similar wrong act of your own there is; for instance, to esteem money or pleasure or glory as goods, and so on with each kind. For if you attend to this, you will quickly forget your anger, when it occurs to you at the same time that he is compelled, for what else can he do? Alternatively, if you can, remove what in him is subject to compulsion.

31. When you see Satyrion, Eutyches, or Hymen, picture a follower of Socrates; or an Euphrates, when you see Eutychion or Silvanus; an Alciphron, when you see Tropaeophorus; and a Crito or Xenophon, when you see Severus.* So when you look at yourself, picture one of the Caesars, and in every case picture a parallel. Then let the thought strike you in the same moment: 'Where are they all? Nowhere, or we know not where.' For in this way you will continually see that man's life is smoke and nothingness,* especially if you remind yourself that what has once changed will be no more in infinite Time. Why then are you bothered? Why not satisfied to pass through this brief moment ordering your ways? What kind of material condition and station are you running away from? What is it all except a school of exercise* for a reason which has exactly and scientifically looked into what life contains? Wait, therefore, until you assimilate even these things to yourself, as a strong stomach assimilates any food and a bright fire* turns whatever you throw into it to flame and light.

32. Don't let it be possible for anyone to say of you truthfully that you are not simple and good, but let him be a liar who thinks any of these things about you. And this entirely rests with you;

for who prevents your being good and simple? Only make up your mind not to go on living,* if you are not like that, for Reason, too, disowns one who is not like that.

33. What is the soundest thing that can be done or said in a given material condition? For whatever this may be, you are able to do or say it, and you are not to make the excuse that you are prevented. You will never cease groaning until you feel that to act appropriately to man's constitution in any material condition which occurs to you or befalls you is for you what luxury is to the sensualist. For you should regard as an indulgence whatever you can achieve in accord with your own nature, and this you can achieve everywhere. Now the roller is not allowed everywhere to be moved according to its own natural movement, nor are water, fire, and the rest, which are governed by natural law or life without reason—for there are many things which separate them and resist them. Mind and reason are able to move through any thing that opposes, as their nature and their will prescribe. Put before your eyes this ease with which reason will prove to be carried through all things (as fire moves upwards, a stone down, a roller on a slope)* and ask for nothing more, for the remaining obstacles are either of the lifeless body or else do not overwhelm it or do any harm at all without the judgement and the consent of reason itself.

For mark you, were it not so, the man affected would have become evil at once; at all events in all other constituted things whatever is affected itself becomes worse because of any evil which happens to it, whereas in this case, if one may so put it, a man becomes better and more laudable by right use of circumstances. And generally, remember that nothing harms the natural citizen which does not harm the city and nothing harms the city which does not harm the law. Now none of what are called strokes of bad luck harms the law: wherefore, not harming the law, it harms neither city nor citizen.

34.* For one bitten by true doctrines even the briefest and most familiar saying is reminder enough to dispel sorrow and fear, for instance:

'leaves,
the wind scatters some on the face of the ground;
like unto them are the children of men.'*

Yes, 'leaves' too are your children, and 'leaves' those whose
voices shout and applaud convincingly or on the contrary curse
you or blame and rail beneath their breath; 'leaves' too even
those who will receive and hand on your fame hereafter. For they
all 'shoot in the season of spring'; then the wind has thrown them
down and the woodland 'bears others' in their stead. Brief life is
the common portion of all, yet you avoid and pursue each thing
as though it will be for everlasting. A little while and you will
close your eyes, and now another will be lamenting* him who
carried you out.

35. The healthy eye should be able to look at every object of
sight, and not to say: 'I wish it were green', for this is what a man
does who has ophthalmia. The healthy ear and nose must be
ready for every object of hearing or smell, and the healthy
stomach must be disposed to every kind of nourishment as the
mill is ready for everything which it is made to grind. Accordingly
the healthy understanding too must be ready for all circumstances; but that which says: 'may my children be kept safe'
or 'may all men praise whatever I do', is the eye looking for green
or the teeth for what is tender.

36. No one is so fortunate but that when he is dying some will
be at his bedside welcoming the evil that is coming to him. Was
he earnest and wise; perhaps there will be someone at the end to
say of him: 'we shall breathe more freely now this schoolmaster
has gone; he was not hard on any of us, but I could feel he was
tacitly condemning us.' So much for the earnest man;* but in our
own case what a number of other things there are for which
many want to be rid of us. You will think then of this as you die
and will depart more easily, thinking to yourself: 'I am going
away from the kind of life in which even my fellow men, for
whom I laboured, prayed, and thought so much, even they wish
me to go away, hoping perhaps for some relief by my death.'
Why then should one hold on to a longer stay in this world? Do

not, however, on this account leave them with less kindness, but preserve your own character, friendly and well disposed and propitious; and again do not go as if you were being torn away, but as for a man who has a quiet end the soul slips easily from its casing, so should your departure be from them. For it was Nature who bound you and united you to them, and now she sets you free. I am set free from men who are certainly my kinsfolk, yet I do not resist and I go under no compulsion. For this, too, is one of the things which are according to Nature.

37. Accustom yourself in the case of whatever is done by anyone, so far as possible to inquire within yourself: 'to what end does this man do this?' And begin with yourself and first examine yourself.

38. Remember that what is hidden within you controls the strings;* that is activity, that is life, that, if one may say so, is the man. Never occupy your imagination besides with the body which encloses you like a vessel and these organs which are moulded round you. They are like an axe, only differing as being attached to the body. For, indeed, these parts are of no more use without the cause which moves or checks them than the shuttle to the weaver, the pen to the writer or the whip to the man who holds the reins.

BOOK XI

1. The properties of the rational soul: it is conscious of itself, it moulds itself, makes of itself whatever it will, the fruit which it bears it gathers itself (whereas others gather the fruits of the field and what in animals corresponds to fruit), it achieves its proper end, wherever the close of life comes upon it; if any interruption occur, its whole action is not rendered incomplete as is the case in the dance or a play and similar arts, but in every scene of life* and wherever it may be overtaken, it makes what it proposed to itself complete and entire, so that it can say: 'I have what is my own.'

Moreover, it goes over the whole Universe and the surrounding void and surveys its shape,* reaches out into the boundless extent of time, embraces and ponders the periodic rebirth* of the Whole and understands that those who come after us will behold nothing new nor did those who came before us behold anything greater, but in a way the man of forty years, if he have any understanding at all, has seen all that has been and that will be by reason of its uniformity. A property, too, of the rational soul is love of one's neighbour, truth, self-reverence and to honour nothing more than itself; and this last is a property of law also; accordingly right principle and the principle of justice differ not at all.

2.* You will despise joyous song and the dance and the combat-at-arms if you disintegrate the tuneful phrase into every one of its notes, and ask yourself about each whether you are its servant; for you will be ashamed. And so you will be if you do what corresponds in the case of the dance in respect of each movement or pose, and the same also in the case of the combat-at-arms. Generally then, excepting virtue and its effects, remember to have recourse to the several parts and by analysis to go on to despise them, and to apply the same process to life as a whole.

3. How admirable is the soul which is ready and resolved, if it must this moment be released from the body, to be either extinguished or scattered or to persist. This resolve, too, must arise from a specific decision.* not out of sheer opposition like the Christians,* but after reflection and with dignity, and so as to convince others, without histrionic display.

4. Have I done a neighbourly act? I am thereby benefited. Let this always be ready to your mind, and nowhere desist.

5. What is your art? To be good. But how is this done except by principles of thought, concerned both with Universal Nature and with man's individual constitution?

6.* First of all tragedies were put on the stage to remind you of what comes to pass and that it is Nature's law for things to happen like that, and that you are not to make what charmed you on the stage a heavy burden on the world's greater stage.* For you see that those events are bound to have that ending and that even those endure them who have cried aloud: 'Alas! Alas! Cithaeron'. There are also valuable sayings in the dramatists; an especially famous one, for instance:

> Were the gods careless of my sons and me,
> Yet there is reason here,

and again:

> Man must not vent his passion on mere things,

or:

> Life, like ripe corn, must to the sickle yield,

and the many others of the same sort.

After Tragedy was introduced the Old Comedy,* which through its instructive frankness and its reminder by actual plainness of language to avoid vanity was not without profit, and this directness Diogenes* also adopted with a somewhat similar object. After the Old, observe what the Middle Comedy was like and afterwards with what end the New Comedy was adopted, passing little by little into a love of technique based on imitation.

It is recognized that there are profitable sayings of these authors also, but after all what was the object to which the whole aim of such poetry and drama looked?

7.* How vividly it strikes you that no other calling in life is so fitted for the practice of philosophy as this in which you now find yourself.

8.* A branch cut off from the bough it belonged to cannot but be cut off also from the whole tree. Similarly a man, if severed from a single man, has fallen away from society as a whole. Now in the case of a branch, it is cut off by another agency, whereas man by his own act divides himself from his neighbour, when he hates him and turns from him, yet he does not realize that at the same time he has severed himself from the whole Commonwealth. Only there is this singular gift of Zeus who brought society together, that we are enabled to join again with the man we belong to, and again to become complements of the Whole. Yet, if it is often repeated, the effect of such separation is to make what separates difficult to unite and to restore. Generally speaking, too, the branch which originally grew with the tree and shared its transpiration, by remaining with it, is different from the branch which is engrafted again after being cut off, whatever gardeners may say.

'Grow together with them but do not share their doctrines.'

9. Just as those who oppose you as you progress in agreement with right principle will not be able to divert you from sound conduct, so do not let them force you to abandon your kindness towards them; but be equally on your guard in both respects, in steady judgement and behaviour as well as in gentleness towards those who try to hinder you or are difficult in other ways. For to be hard upon them is a weakness just as much as to abandon your course and to give in, from fright; for both are equally deserters from their post, the man who is in a panic as well as the man who is alienated from his natural kinsman and friend.

10. 'No Nature is inferior to Art',* for the crafts imitate natural things. If then this be true, the Nature which is the most

perfect of all natures and all inclusive would not fall short of technical inventiveness. Moreover, all crafts create the lower in the interests of the higher, wherefore the Universal Nature does the same. And so from her is the birth of Justice, and from Justice the rest of the virtues have their existence; for Justice will not be preserved if we are concerned for indifferent objects or are easily deceived by them or are liable to stumble or to change.

11. The objects whose pursuit or avoidance disturbs your peace do not come to you, but in a measure you go to them. Let your judgement at all events about them be untroubled and they will remain unmoved, and you will be seen neither to pursue nor to avoid them.

12. The sphere* of the soul is true to its own form, when it is neither extended in any way nor contracted inwards; when it is neither scattered nor dies down, but is lighted by the light whereby it sees the truth of all things and the truth within itself.

13. Will any man despise me? Let him see to it. But I will see to it that I may not be found doing or saying anything that deserves to be despised. Will he hate me? Let him see to it. But I will be kind and well-disposed to every man and ready to show him what is overlooked, not reproachfully nor as though I were displaying forbearance, but genuinely and generously like the famous Phocion,* if he was not in fact pretending. For the inward parts ought to be like that, and a man ought to be seen by the gods to be neither disposed to indignation nor complaining. For what harm is there to you if you are yourself at the moment doing the thing which is appropriate to your nature and accepting what is at this moment in season for Universal Nature, as a human being intent upon the common benefit being somehow realized?

14. They despise one another, yet they flatter one another; they want to get above one another and yet bow down to one another.

15.* How rotten and crafty is the man who says: 'I have made up my mind to deal plainly with you.' What are you about, my friend? This preface is not necessary. The intention will reveal itself, it ought to be graven on the forehead; the tone of voice should give that sound at once; the intention should shine out in the eyes at once, as the beloved at once reads the whole in the glances of lovers. The simple and good man ought to be entirely such, like the unsavoury man, that those who stand by detect him at once, whether he will or not, as soon as he comes near. But the affectation of simplicity is like a razor;* nothing is uglier than the wolf's profession of friendship, avoid that above all. The good and simple and kind has these qualities in his eyes and they are not hidden.

16. Live constantly the highest life. This power is in a man's soul, if he is indifferent to what is indifferent; and he will be so, if he regard every one of these indifferent objects as a whole and in its parts, remembering that none of them creates in us a conception about itself nor even comes to us, but they are motionless, and it is we who create judgements about them and so to speak inscribe them on ourselves; and yet we need not inscribe them and, if we do so unconsciously, we can wipe them off again at once. Remember, too, that attention to this kind of thing will last but a little while and, after that, life will have reached its close. And yet what difficulty do these things present? If they are what Nature wills, rejoice in them and you will find them easy: if they are not, look for what your own nature wills and hasten to this, even should it bring you no glory; for every man is pardoned if he seeks his own good.

17. What the origin of each experience is and the material condition of each; what it is changing into and what it will be like when it has changed, and that it will suffer no injury by the change.

18.* First, what is my position in regard to others and how we came into the world for one another; and, to put it in a different way, that I was born to protect them, as the ram protects his flocks or the bull his herd. Then, going further back, proceed from the truth that, unless the Universe is mere atoms, it is Nature which administers the Whole and, granted this, the lower are in the interests of the higher, the higher for one another.

Secondly, what creatures they are at board and in bed and so on, and above all what kind of compulsion they are under because of their opinions, and with what arrogance they do what they do.

Thirdly, that, if they do what is right, you ought not to complain, but if what is wrong, clearly they act involuntarily and in ignorance—for as every soul is unwilling to be deprived of the truth, so is it unwilling not to be related to every man according to his worth; at any rate they resent it, if they are spoken of as unjust, inconsiderate, overreaching, in a word as wrong-doers in regard to their neighbours.

Fourthly, that you yourself also often do wrong and are another such as they are, and that, even if you do abstain from some kinds of wrong action, at all events you have at least a proclivity to them, though cowardice or tenderness for your good name or some similar bad motive keeps you from offences like theirs.

Fifthly, that you are not even sure that they actually do wrong; for many actions are done to serve a given purpose and, generally, one must ascertain much before making a certainly correct decision upon a neighbour's conduct.

Sixthly, when you are highly indignant or actually suffering, that man's life is but a moment, and in a little we are one and all laid low in death.

Seventhly, that it is not what they do that troubles us, for that lies in their own governing selves, but it is our judgements about them. Very well then, remove your judgement about the supposed hurt and make up your mind to dismiss it, and your anger is gone. How then will you remove it? By reflecting that what hurts you is not morally bad; for unless what is morally bad is alone hurtful, it follows of necessity that you also do much wrong and become a brigand and a shifty character.

Eighthly, how much more grievous are what fits of anger and the consequent sorrows bring than the actual things are which produce in us those angry fits and sorrows.

Ninthly, that gentleness is invincible, if it be genuine and not sneering or hypocritical.* For what can the most insolent do to you, if you continue gentle to him, and, if opportunity allows, mildly admonish him and quietly show him a better way at the very moment when he attempts to do you injury: 'No, my child; we came into the world for other ends. It is not I that am harmed, but you are harmed, my child.' And point out with tact and on general grounds that this is so, that not even bees act like that nor the many creatures that are by nature gregarious. But you must not do it ironically or as if finding fault, but affectionately and not feeling the sting in your soul, nor as if you were lecturing him* or desired some bystander to admire you, but even if others are present, just in the way you would address him if you were alone.

Remember these nine brief prescriptions, taking them as a gift from the Muses, and begin at last to be a human being, while life remains. And be as much on your guard against flattering them as against being angry with them, for both faults are unsocial and tend to injury. And in your angry fits have the maxim ready that it is not passion that is manly, but that what is kind and gentle as it is more human so is it more manly, and that this is the character which has strength and sinews and fortitude, not that which is indignant and displeased; for as this is nearer to imperturbability so it is nearer to power; and as grief is a mark of weakness, so also is anger, for both have been wounded and have surrendered to the wound.

And, if you will, receive a tenth gift from the leader of the nine Muses, to wit that it is madness to require bad men not to do wrong, for it is aiming at the impossible.* Still, to permit them to be such to others and to require them not to do wrong to yourself is to be unfeeling and tyrannical.

19. You are especially to guard unremittingly against four moods of the governing self, and to wipe them out whenever you detect them, using in each case the following remedies: this imagination is not necessary; this is a solvent of society; this which you are about to say is not from yourself, and not to speak from yourself you must consider to be most incongruous.

The fourth thing that will cause you to reproach yourself is that this ensues from your more divine part* being overcome and yielding to the less honourable and mortal portion, the body and its gross pleasures.

20. Your element of spirit and all the element of fire that is mingled in you, in spite of their natural upward tendency, nevertheless obey the ordering of the Whole and are held forcibly in the compounded body in this region of the earth. Once more, all the elements of earth and of water in you, in spite of their downward tendency, are nevertheless lifted up and keep to a position which is not natural to them. In this way then even the elements are obedient to the Whole and, when they are stationed at a given point, remain there by compulsion until once more the signal for their dissolution is made from the other world.*

Is it not then monstrous that only your mind-element should disobey and be dissatisfied with its station? Yet nothing is imposed upon it that does violence to it, only what is in accord with its own nature, and still it does not tolerate this, but is carried in a reverse direction. For movement towards acts of injustice and habitual vice, towards wrath and sorrow and fear, is nothing else but a movement of severance from Nature. Moreover, when the governing self is discontented with any circumstance, then, too, it deserts its proper station, for it is constituted for holiness and the service of God no less than for just dealing with man. For these relations belong in kind to good fellowship, or rather are even more to be reverenced than just dealings.

21. 'He who has not one and the same aim in life is unable to remain one and the same through all his life.' The saying is incomplete unless you add what sort of aim it should be. For as the conception of all the variety of goods which the majority of men fancy in any way to be good is not the same, but only the conception of certain of the kinds of goods, namely the general goods, so the aim to be set before oneself must be the social aim, that is the aim of the Commonwealth. For he who directs every private impulse to this will make all his actions uniform and because of this will always be the same man.

22. The mountain mouse and the town mouse,* and the fright and scurry of the latter.

23. Socrates* used to call the opinions of the multitude like other things: 'Bogies', things to frighten children.

24.* The Spartans used to put seats for visitors at their entertainments in the shade, and to seat themselves wherever they found room.

25. Socrates' message to Perdiccas* to excuse a visit to his court; 'to avoid', he said, 'coming to a most unfortunate end, that is, to be treated handsomely and not to have the power to return it.'

26. The writings of the school of Epicurus lay down the injunction to remind oneself continually of one of those who practised virtue in the days gone by.*

27.* The Pythagoreans say: 'Look up to the sky before morning breaks', to remind ourselves of beings who always in the same relations and in the same way accomplish their work, and of their order, purity, and nakedness; for a star has no veil.*

28. What a man Socrates was in his undergarment only, when Xanthippe* took his upper garment and went out; and what he said to the friends who were shocked and retired when they saw him in that dress.

29. In writing and reciting you will not be a master before you have been a pupil. This is much more true of living.

30.* 'You are a slave by nature: reason is not your part.'

31.* 'And my dear heart laughed within.'

32.* 'Virtue they will reproach, mocking her with harsh words.'

33.* Only a madman expects a fig in winter; such is he who expects a child when it is no longer permitted.

34. Epictetus used to say that, as you kissed your child, you

should say in your heart: 'tomorrow maybe you will die'. 'Those are words of ill omen.' 'No,' he replied, 'nothing that means an act of Nature is of evil omen, or it would be a bad omen to say that the corn has been reaped.'

35. The unripe grape, the ripe bunch, the dried raisin, all are changes; not to nothing, but to what at this moment is nothing.

36.* 'There is no robber of the will,' as Epictetus says.

37.* He said too: 'you must find out an art of assent, and keep your attention fixed in the sphere of the impulses, that they may be controlled by reservation, be social, and in proportion to value; and you must wholly abstain from desire and employ aversion in regard to nothing that is not in our own control.

38. 'So we are contending,' he said, 'for no ordinary prize, but for whether we are to be sane or insane.'

39.* Socrates used to say: 'What do you want? To have souls of rational or irrational beings?' 'Rational.' 'What rational beings, sound or inferior?' 'Sound.' 'Why don't you seek them?' 'Because we have them.' 'Why then do you fight and disagree?'

BOOK XII

1. It is in your power to secure at once all the objects which you dream of reaching by a roundabout path, if you will be fair to yourself: that is, if you will leave all the past behind, commit the future to Providence, and direct the present, and that alone, to Holiness and Justice. Holiness, to love your dispensation—for Nature brought it to you and you to it; Justice, freely and without circumlocution both to speak the truth and to do the things that are according to law and according to worth. And be not hampered by another's evil, his judgement, or his words, much less by the sensation of the flesh that has formed itself about you—let the part affected look to itself. If then, when you arrive at last at your final exit, resigning all else, you honour your governing self alone and the divine element within you, if what you dread is not that some day you will cease to live, but rather never to begin at all to live with Nature, you will be a man worthy of the Universe that gave you birth, and will cease to be a stranger in your own country, surprised by what is coming to pass every day, as at something you did not look to see, and absorbed in this thing or in that.

2. God beholds the governing selves of all men stripped of their material vessels and coverings and dross; for with His own mind alone He touches only what has flowed and been drawn from Himself into these selves. You, too, if you make it your habit to do this, will rid yourself of your exceeding unrest. For it would be strange that one who does not behold the poor envelope of flesh should yet lose his time in admiring dress and dwelling and reputation, and all such trappings and masquerade.

3. There are three things of which you are compounded: body, vital spirit, mind.* Two of these are your own in so far as you must take care of them, but only the third is in the strict sense your own. So, if you separate from yourself, namely from

your mind, all that others do or say, all that you yourself did or said, all that troubles you in the future, all that as part of the bodily envelope or natural spirit attaches to you without your will, and all that the external circumfluent vortex whirls round, so that your mind power, freed from the chain of necessity, lives purified and released by itself—doing what is just, willing what comes to pass, and speaking what is true; if you separate, I say, from this governing self what is attached to it by sensibility, and what of time is hereafter or has gone by, and make yourself like the sphere of Empedocles,* 'rounded, rejoicing in the solitude which is about it', and practise only to live the life you are living, that is the present, then you will have it in your power at least to live out the time that is left until you die, untroubled and with kindness and reconciled with your own good Spirit.

4. I often wonder how it is that everyone loves himself more than all the world and yet takes less account of his own judgement of himself than of the judgement of the world. At all events, if a god appeared to him or some wise master and bade him think and contemplate nothing within himself without at the same time speaking it out loud, he would not tolerate it even for a single day. Thus we respect whatever our neighbours will think about us more highly than we respect ourselves.

5.* How was it that the gods, who ordered all things aright and with love to man, overlooked this one thing only, that among mortal men some altogether good, who had, so to speak, most commerce with the Godhead, and by holy acts and solemn rites had grown in the highest degree familiar with Him, should, once dead, never come into being again but be entirely extinguished?

Now, if indeed it is so, be certain of this that, if it ought to have been otherwise, the gods would have made it so; for were it just, it would also be possible, and were it accordant with Nature, Nature would have brought it about. Therefore from its not being so, if indeed it is not so, you should believe that it ought not to come to pass. For you yourself see that, by questioning thus, you are arguing a point of justice with God. Now we should not be debating thus with the gods unless they were most good and most just; and if this is true, they would not have permitted any part of the ordered world they govern to be unjustly and unreasonably neglected.

6. Practise even the things which you despair of achieving. For even the left hand, which for other uses is slow from want of practice, has a stronger hold upon the bridle rein than the right; for it has been practised in this.

7. What ought one to be like both in body and soul, when overtaken by death; the brevity of life; the gulf of Time hereafter and gone by; the weakness of all matter.

8.* Consider the causes of reality stripped of their covering; the relations of your actions; the nature of pain, pleasure, death, fame; who is not the author of his own unrest; how none is hindered by his neighbour; that all things are what we judge them to be.

9. In the use of principles model yourself on the boxer, not the gladiator. The one puts away the sword he uses and takes it up again; the other has his hand always, and need but clench it.

10. See facts as they really are, distinguishing their matter, cause, relation.

11. How large a liberty man has to do nothing other than what God will commend, and to welcome all that God assigns to him as a consequence of Nature.

12. The gods must not be blamed; for they do no wrong, willingly or unwillingly; nor human beings; for they do no wrong except unwillingly. Therefore no one is to be blamed.

13. How ridiculous and like a stranger to the world is he who is surprised at any one of the events of life.

14–15. Either the Necessity of destiny and an order none may transgress, or Providence that hears intercession, or an ungoverned welter without a purpose.* If then a Necessity which none may transgress, why do you resist? If a Providence admitting intercession, make yourself worthy of assistance from the

Godhead. If an undirected welter, be glad that in so great a flood of waves you have yourself within you* a directing mind; and, if the flood carry you away, let it carry away flesh, vital-spirit, the rest of you, for your mind it shall not carry away. Does the light of the lamp shine and not lose its radiance until it be put out, and shall truth and justice and temperance be put out in you before the end?*

16. In the case of one who gives the impression that he did wrong, how do I know that this was a wrong? And, if he certainly did wrong, how do I know that he was not condemning himself, and so what he did was like tearing his own face? One who wants an evil man not to do wrong is like a man who wants a fig-tree not to produce its acrid juice in the figs, and infants not to cry, and a horse not to neigh, and whatever else is inevitable. With that kind of disposition what else can he do? Very well then, if you are man enough, cure this disposition.

17–18. If it is not right, don't do it: if it is not true, don't say it. Let your impulse be to see always and entirely what precisely it is which is creating an impression in your imagination, and to open it up by dividing it into cause, matter, relation, and into the period within which it will be bound to have ceased.

19. Perceive at last that you have within yourself something stronger and more divine than the things which create your passions and make a downright puppet of you. What is my consciousness at this instant? Fright, suspicion, appetite? Some similar evil state?

20. First, do nothing aimlessly nor without relation to the end. Secondly, relate your action to no other end except the good of human fellowship.

21. A little while and you will be nobody and nowhere, nor will anything which you now behold exist, nor one of those who are now alive. Nature's law is that all things change and turn, and pass away, so that in due order different things may come to be.

22. All things are what we judge them to be, and that rests

with you. Put away, therefore, when you will, the judgement; and, as though you had doubled the headland, there is calm, 'all smoothly strewn and a waveless bay'.*

23. Any single activity you choose, which ceases in due season, suffers no evil because it has ceased, neither has he, whose activity it was, suffered any evil merely because his activity has ceased. Similarly, therefore, the complex of all activities, which is man's life, suffers no evil merely because it has ceased, provided that it ceases in due season, nor is he badly used who in due season brings his series of activities to a close. But the season and the term Nature assigns—sometimes the individual nature, as in old age, but in any event Universal Nature, for by the changes of her parts the whole world continues ever young and in her prime. Now what tends to the advantage of the Whole is ever altogether lovely and in season; therefore for each individual the cessation of his life is no evil, for it is no dishonour to him, being neither of his choosing nor without relation to the common good: rather is it good, because it is in due season for the Whole, benefiting it and itself benefited by it. For thus is he both carried by God, who is borne along the same course with God, and of purpose borne to the same ends as God.

24. These three thoughts keep always ready for use: First, in what you do that your act be not without purpose and not otherwise than Right itself would have done, and that outward circumstances depend either on chance or Providence; but neither is chance to be blamed, nor Providence arraigned. The second, to remember the nature of each individual from his conception to his first breath, and from his first breath until he gives back the breath of life, and the mere elements of which he is compounded and into which he is resolved. The third, to realize that if you could be suddenly caught up into the air and could look down upon human life and see all its variety you would disdain it, seeing at the same time how great a company of beings,* in the air and in the aether, encompasses you, and that however often you were caught up, you would see the same things— uniformity, transience: *these* are the objects of your pride.*

25. Cast out the judgement; you are saved. Who then hinders your casting it out?

26. Whenever you feel something hard to bear, you have forgotten (*a*) that all comes to pass according to the Nature of the Whole, (*b*) that the wrong is not your own but another's, further (*c*) that all that is coming to pass always did, always will, and does now everywhere thus come to pass, (*d*) the great kinship of man with all mankind, for the bond of kind is not blood nor the seed of life, but mind. You have forgotten, moreover (*e*), that every individual's mind is of God and has flowed from that other world, (*f*) that nothing is a man's own, but even his child, his body, and his vital spirit itself have come from that other world, (*g*) that all is judgement, (*h*) that every man lives only the present life and this is what he is losing.

27. Continually run over in mind men who were highly indignant at some event; men who attained the greatest heights of fame or disaster or enmity or of any kind of fortune whatever. Then pause and think: 'Where is it all now?' Smoke and ashes* and a tale that is told, or not so much as a tale. And see that all such as this occurs to you together: Fabius Catullinus, for instance, in his country retreat, Lusius Lupus in his gardens, Stertinius at Baiae, Tiberius in Capri, and Velius Rufus*—and generally some idiosyncrasy coupled with vanity; and how cheap is all that man strains to get, and how much wiser it were, with the material granted to you, to present yourself just, temperate, obedient to the gods in all simplicity; for pride smouldering under a cover of humility is the most grievous pride of all.

28. To those who ask the question:* 'Where have you seen the gods, or whence have you apprehended that they exist, that you thus worship them?' First, they are visible even to the eyes; secondly, I have not seen my own soul and yet I honour it; and so, too, with the gods, from my experiences every instant of their power, from these I apprehend that they exist and I do them reverence.

29. The security of life is to see each object in itself, in its

entirety, its material, its cause; with the whole heart to do just acts and to speak the truth. What remains except to enjoy life, joining one good thing to another, so as to leave not even the smallest interval unfilled?

30*. One light of the Sun, even though it be sundered by walls, by mountains, by a myriad other barriers. One common Matter, even though it be sundered in a myriad individual bodies. One vital spirit, even though it be sundered in a myriad natural forms and individual outlines. One intelligent spirit, even though it appears to be divided. Now of the things we have named the other parts, for instance animal spirits and material bodies without sense, are even unrelated to one another; yet even them the principle of unity and the gravitation of like to like holds together. But understanding has a peculiar property, it tends to its fellow and combines therewith, and the feeling of fellowship is not sundered.

31. What more do you ask? To go on in your mere existence? Well then, to enjoy your senses, your impulses? To wax and then to wane? To employ your tongue, your intelligence? Which of these do you suppose is worth your longing? But if each and all are to be despised, go forward to the final act, to follow Reason, that is God. But to honour those other ends, to be distressed because death will rob one of them, conflicts with this end.

32. What a fraction of infinite and gaping time has been assigned to every man; for very swiftly it vanishes in the eternal; and what a fraction of the whole of matter, and what a fraction of the whole of the life Spirit. On what a small clod, too, of the whole earth you creep. Pondering all these things, imagine nothing to be great but this: to act as your own nature guides, to suffer what Universal Nature brings.

33. How is the governing self employing itself? For therein is everything. The rest are either within your will or without it, ashes and smoke.

34.* This is a stirring call to disdain of death, that even those who judge pleasure to be good and pain evil, nevertheless disdain death.

35. For him whose sole good is what is in due season, who counts it all one to render according to right reason more acts or fewer, and to whom it is no matter whether he beholds the world a longer or a shorter time—for him even death has lost its terrors.

36. Mortal man, you have been a citizen in this great City;* what does it matter to you whether for five or fifty years? For what is according to its laws is equal for every man. Why is it hard, then, if Nature who brought you in, and no despot nor unjust judge, sends you out of the City—as though the master of the show, who engaged an actor,* were to dismiss him from the stage? 'But I have not spoken my five acts, only three.' 'What you say is true, but in life three acts are the whole play.' For He determines the perfect whole, the cause yesterday of your composition, to-day of your dissolution; you are the cause of neither. Leave the stage, therefore, and be reconciled, for He also who lets his servant depart is reconciled.

APPENDIX

A Selection from the Correspondence of Marcus Cornelius Fronto and Marcus Aurelius

Introductory Note

Fronto was born in Cirta, in North Africa, probably about AD 95, and was thus some 25 years older than Marcus Aurelius. He was renowned as an orator and a man of letters in the mid-second century AD. He also enjoyed a highly successful public career, and was consul in AD 143. From late 138 or early 139 he served as tutor to the future emperors Marcus and Verus. Although Marcus speaks briefly of him in the *Meditations* (i. 11), and some sketchy anecdotes illustrating his literary tastes, together with some of his *bons mots*, are preserved in the work of Aulus Gellius, concrete evidence about Fronto the man was largely lacking until the beginning of the nineteenth century, when the remnants of a large number of letters were discovered, in a disorderly and fragmentary state, largely overwritten by other scribes partially erasing and reusing the various manuscripts at a later date (such overwriting produces what is known as a *palimpsest*). This collection includes letters by Fronto to many addressees but especially to Marcus Aurelius. The text also contains many replies from Marcus and an assortment of letters by other hands. These letters are often incomplete, frequently indecipherable, and although some are datable from internal evidence, they are not arranged in an accurate chronological sequence, and the reconstruction of date and circumstances is often wholly speculative. On a few occasions it is even unclear whether Marcus or Verus is actually the addressee in question. In short, the discovery of these letters, while an exciting illustration of the continuing progress possible in classical scholarship, often raised insoluble problems; and the quality of Fronto's style and thought

gravely disappointed many who had accepted antiquity's verdict
on him as a second Cicero. Despite all uncertainties and dis-
appointments, however, the correspondence has yielded much
interesting material for the social historian, and also makes
some contribution to the study of literary history, especially of
the archaizing movement in vogue at the time of Fronto's active
literary career. As for Marcus, the letters give us an attractive insight into the honourable and generous affections of the emperor,
while also providing confirmation of his serious and sometimes
severe nature. The datable letters span a period from about 139
(when Marcus was 18 and studying rhetoric with Fronto) to
Fronto's death, which probably occurred around the year 167, by
which time Marcus had been emperor for seven years. Not all the
material in the collection consists of letters in the strict sense.
There are a number of longer essays which may have been couched in epistolary form and sent to their recipient, but which seem
less private and may also be intended for publication: we have
fragments, for instance, of the preliminaries or prologue to a
history which Fronto began but seems not to have completed, re-
counting the wars of Lucius Verus in Parthia. Even the moving
fragment on the premature death of his grandson (below, pp.
140–43) is a polished piece and may be intended for a wider
public; similarly, Quintilian, also a tutor of princes and a
distinguished rhetorical theorist, prefaced to the sixth book of his
great treatise on oratory a lament, no doubt equally genuine, for
the premature death of his son.

The extracts translated here are chosen primarily to give some
idea of Fronto's personality and his relations with Marcus,
secondly with a view to variety of date and style. They are
arranged as far as possible in chronological order, though as
already indicated this is often controversial. Triple dots (. . .)
indicate gaps in the text, not ancient punctuation. The translation is based on the edition by M. P. J. van den Hout (Leiden,
1954), and the page references given in the title of each letter are
to this edition. At a late stage I was able to consult van den Hout's
revised edition, published by the Teubner Library, Leipzig 1988:
this offers a more up-to-date and fuller apparatus, an extensive

bibliography, and an annotated table of chronology. Although the new edition is more informative, the text appears to be substantially unchanged, and it should be possible to use this translation with van den Hout's 1988 edition as easily as with his earlier text. References to the page-numbers of both editions are given in the table on p. 192. A brief introduction to each letter is given in the Explanatory Notes, pp. 184 ff.

For a full translation of all the correspondence, the reader may consult the version by C. R. Haines, in the Loeb Classical Library (2 volumes, Heinemann, Cambridge Mass. and London, 1919–20). The second volume of that edition also includes a useful appendix containing other references to or quotations from Fronto in ancient sources.

1 pp. 44–5. 140s AD. Marcus to Fronto.

To my master.

During this space of time I have received two letters from you. In the first of these you rebuked me and showed that I had composed an extravagant aphorism, but in the other you took pains to preserve my enthusiasm through praise. But I swear to you by my own safety, my mother's and your own, that more joy arose in my heart in response to the first letter, and that I more often exclaimed as I read: how lucky I am! Somebody may ask 'are you so lucky, just because you have someone who can teach you how to write a *mot* with greater skill, clarity, brevity, and polish?' That is not why I claim the title of a lucky man. What then is the reason? It is because I learn from you how to speak the truth; and that ability, to tell the truth, is a hard task indeed, for men and gods alike. No oracle is so truthful that it fails to include some ambiguity or oblique or puzzling expression in which the less foresighted enquirer may become entrammelled, and having supposed that the oracle is according to his wishes, may realize after time and trouble that he has been trapped. But oracular consultations are profitable, and of course the custom is to excuse such things as merely pious fraud and flummery. But your criticisms or indeed the penalties you exact show the true way at once without trickery or invented words. So I would also be able to pay you thanks if you teach me both to speak the truth and to hear it myself. Let a double reward be paid, then; you, though, will do your best to make sure that I cannot pay it. If you don't want to receive any return for your teaching, how can I pay you back fairly and equally, except by devotion? But I (impious fellow that I am) preferred you to be disturbed by my excessive attention [?] . . .

Farewell, good and best orator; I rejoice that I have found you to be so. My lady mother sends her greetings.

2 pp. 26–7. August 143. Marcus to Fronto.

M. Aurelius Caesar to his dear consul and his master, greeting! If the Greeks of old ever wrote anything of the quality of your speech, then those who know will be aware of it; but as for me, if it is right for me to say this, I never observed Marcus Porcius (Cato)* dealing out denunciations as finely as you have dealt out praise. O if only my lord could be sufficiently praised, he would certainly have been so by you! 'But that cannot now be.' A man might more easily imitate Pheidias,* or Apelles,* or most difficult of all Demosthenes,* or Cato himself, than this work of yours with all its polish and marks of painstaking care. I have never read anything more refined, anything more in the ancient style, anything more elegant, anything more Latin. What a happy man you are, endowed with such eloquence! What a happy man I am, entrusted to such a master! O what argumentation! What organization! What neatness, what charm, what taste, what choice of words, what glitter, what point, what graces, what devoted practice you put in, what—everything! May I never prosper, if the day does not come when a staff shall be placed in your hand, a coronet set upon your head, a platform established for you, and then the herald would summon us all—why do I say 'us'? What I mean is all those who love words and all your learned speakers: you would guide each one of them with your rod, rebuke them with your words. As for me, I have no fear of such admonition as yet; there are still many reasons for me to make my way into your school.

I send you this with the utmost haste; for when I am sending you so amiable a letter from my lord, what need for a more verbose letter from me? And so, fare well, glory of Roman eloquence, bringer of renown to your friends, great phenomenon, most delightful of men, most distinguished of consuls, sweetest of masters.

After this you are to be careful not to tell so many lies about me, particularly in the senate! Your speech made me cringe. O if only for every chapter-head I could give your own head a kiss. 'In your mightiness you have left all mankind behind you.' After reading this speech we study in vain, we strive in vain, we strain our mental sinews in vain against you. Fare well always, sweetest master.

3 pp. 27–8. July/August 143. Marcus to Fronto.

Marcus Caesar greets the most illustrious consul his teacher.

. . . joined by kinship (?) and not subject to guardianship, and besides set in the position in life in which (as Quintus Ennius has it) 'all men give empty counsel and all their words are aimed at pleasure'; in the same vein, there is what Plautus says so splendidly on the same topic in his *Flatterer*:

> Men who give their solemn oath and break it, failing the man who had faith in them, subtle smooth-talkers, men who are closest to the king, who say one thing to the king in their words, but hide different thoughts in their hearts.

For these troubles used to affect only kings, but now there are enough of them, as Naevius has it, 'who would give lip service to the sons of kings, and nod at their words and play the slave's part'. And so it is with good cause, master, that I burn; with good reason have I set one single goal before me, with good reason do I think of one man alone, when pen comes to hand.

In your delightful way you ask to see my hexameters, and if I had them with me, I would have sent them too without delay. My clerk, you know the man I mean, Anicetus, sent none of my written work with me when I set out. For he knows my failing, and was afraid that, if they had passed into my power, I might do what I often have and consign them to the flames. But in fact there was no danger of that in the case of these hexameters. To tell the truth to my dear master, I am besotted with them. I confess that I am busy with them at night, for during the day my time is taken up at the games. And so I do my work less well in the evening, being worn out, but get up half asleep at daybreak. I have, however, put together during this period extracts from sixty books in five volumes—but when you read the word 'sixty', that includes the Novian and Atellan mimes, and Scipio's short speeches, so don't be too horrified at the number!

Since you have mentioned your man Polemo, please don't bring up Horace as well: as far as I'm concerned he is dead and buried along with Pollio.

Fare well, my dearest of friends, fare well my most loving friend, illustrious consul, sweetest master, whom I have not seen for the last two years. Some people claim only two months have intervened, but they are only counting the days. Will the time ever come when I shall see you?

4 pp. 43–4. Undatable between 139 and 161.
Marcus to Fronto.

Greetings, best of masters.

I know that on anybody's birthday friends generally offer up prayers for the one whose birthday it is; but since I love you just as much as I do my own self, I wish to pray for my own felicity on this day, your birthday. And so it is that I call upon all the gods who in any nation bestow their swift and present power upon mankind, who in any part of the world give aid and wield their power through dreams or mysteries or healing power or oracles—each and every one of those gods I summon to hear my prayers, and according to the nature of each prayer, I set myself in the spot from which the god to whose province my prayer pertains may more readily hear it.

Therefore I first scale the citadel of Pergamum and entreat Aesculapius to guide well the good health of my master, and to guard it with all his heart. Thence I diverge to Athens, and appealing to Minerva on bended knee I implore and beg her, if ever I gain any knowledge of literature, to make sure it is from Fronto's lips above all that this knowledge finds its way to a new abode in my breast. Now I revisit Rome, and supplicate the gods of the roadways and those who guard the traveller by sea, begging that all my voyages be accompanied by your present aid, and that I shall never again be so frequently wearied by this vicious longing for you. Last of all, I ask all the gods who reign over all nations, and the very grove itself, which rustles upon the Capitoline mount, to bestow on us the opportunity to celebrate together this day which bore you for me, with you in good health and happy.

Fare well, my sweetest and dearest master. I beg you, take care of your health, so that I may see you when I arrive. My lady mother greets you.

5 pp. 60–1. Undatable between 139 and 161. Marcus to Fronto.

M. Caesar to his teacher M. Fronto, greetings.

After mounting the carriage and saying my farewells to you, we had a reasonably comfortable journey, but did get a little bit of a soaking from some rain. But before we got to the villa, we made a detour of about a mile from the road to visit Anagnia. Then we had a look at the old city there, which despite its tiny size still contains many antiquities, including temples, and holy ceremonies of no common order. There wasn't a corner to be found where there wasn't some sacred building or shrine or temple. They also have many books on linen; that is something which relates to the rituals. Then, when we emerged through the gate, we saw that there was an inscription there, in two places, reading *flamen sume samentum* ('priest, don the samentum'). I asked one of the people of the district what that word meant. According to him, it's a word of the Hernic dialect, meaning a felt covering made from the sacrificial beast's skin, which the priest puts on his cap when he enters the town. We learned from him a good many other things we wanted to know, but the one thing we weren't glad of was that you weren't with us; that was our chief regret.

Now that you have set out, did you make for the Aurelian estate or Campania? Do make sure that you write and tell me that, and also whether you've begun the harvest of the vines, or assembled a massive population of books at your villa; and tell me also whether you miss me—a foolish question on my part, for I am sure you do. Now if you miss me and if you love me, you are to send me regular letters; that soothes and provides me with a curative balm. For I'd ten times rather read your letters than pluck all the vine-shoots of the Massic and Gauran vineyards;* the grapes of Segni are too sour and have excessively acid berries; I'd rather drink that mature than when it's still unfermented. Besides, grapes of that sort are much more satisfactorily eaten when made into raisin-wine than when they are still young; I'd certainly prefer to tread them with my feet rather than chewing them with my teeth! But all the same, let them be gracious and appeased and grant me their kindly pardon for these humorous remarks. Farewell, my dearest fellow, sweetest and most learned, most delightful of masters.

PS. When you see the unfermented wine seething in the vat, remember that longing for you is flowing forth in my heart in just the same way, gushing about and forming a froth! Fare well always.

6 A fragment, p. 36. After 139. Fronto to Marcus.

. . . unless (?) . . . is given dignity by . . . of words, it becomes simply shameless and unchaste. In a word, when you yourself have had to speak in the senate or in the popular assembly, you have never used any word that is somewhat far-fetched, you have never employed any opaque or unfamiliar figure of speech: you showed yourself one who knows that a Caesar's eloquence should be like a trumpet's blast, not a flute's trill; the latter gives forth less noise and is more difficult to catch.

7 pp. 61–2.   140s AD.   Marcus to Fronto.

Greetings, my most venerable master.

We are in good health. Today I pursued my studies from the ninth hour of the night until the second hour of the day (having digested my dinner well);* from the second to the third hour I paced up and down in my sandals in front of my bedchamber; then I put on my outdoor shoes and my military cloak (for those were my instructions for attendance), and off I went to pay morning greetings to my lord [Pius].

We set off hunting, and doughty deeds we did! By hearsay I gather we bagged some boars; I didn't get the chance to see those. Still, we made it up a fairly tough hillside; then in the afternoon we got back home. I settled down to my books; and so with shoes off, clothes set aside, I lingered in bed for a couple of hours. I read Cato's speech 'On the property of Pulchra', and another speech, in which he impeached a tribune. Hey you, you'll be saying to your slave, off with you as quick as you can and bring me those speeches from the library of Apollo. You're sending for them in vain, since those two volumes have come away with me. You'll need to get on the right side of the custodian of Tiberius' library; you'll have to expend some money on this, of which he can give me an equal share when I return to Rome!

But after perusing these speeches I wrote a little something of my own—dreadful stuff, fit for consigning to the powers of Water and Vulcan, god of Fire. 'In truth ill-fortune dogged my pen this day.' It was clearly the frightful little scribbling of a huntsman or a vine-dresser, who were making my room echo with their wild shouts outside; just as hateful and boring as the noise of the court-room cases. Why did I say that? But no, I'm right, for my master is an orator (no mere advocate).

I don't know whether you will think that the fact that I've caught a cold is due to my walking around in sandals in the early hours or to my poor writing. At all events, while I am certainly a man of a generally runny-nosed tendency, today I find myself much more of a sniveller. So I'll pour the oil on my head when I settle down to sleep, since I'm not going to waste a single drop on the oil-lamp, what with the exhaustion that hunting and sneezing have brought about between them.

The best of health to you, my dearest and sweetest master, whom I long to see more (if I dared admit it) than Rome itself.

8 pp. 62–3.   The next day.   Marcus to Fronto.

Greetings, my sweetest master.

We are in good health. I went to sleep rather early last night on account of my little cold, which seems to have died down. So from the eleventh hour of the night until the third of the day I spent some of the time reading parts of Cato's essay *On Agriculture*,* and some of it writing—less dreadfully, thank goodness, than yesterday. Then after paying my respects to my father [Pius], I took a dose of water mixed with honey, keeping it in my mouth and not swallowing, and so I 'tended the throat', an expression I prefer to 'gargled', since it is a phrase in Novius, I think, and found elsewhere too. Once I'd soothed my throat with this treatment I went to see my father and joined him at a sacrifice; after that on to luncheon. What do you think I had to eat? A tiny portion of bread, as I saw the others hogging beans, onions, and fish well-advanced in pregnancy. After that we spent some time on the grape harvest, sweating and shouting away together, and as our author has it, 'left but a few survivors of the harvest, hanging high in the trees'. We made for home at the sixth hour of the day.

I did only a little studying, and what I did do was trivial. Later with my little mother sitting on the couch I had a good natter. My conversation ran along these lines: 'what do you think my dear Fronto is doing at this moment?' Then she would ask: 'what do you think my Gratia is up to?' And I, 'or again, what about our tiny darling little sparrow Gratia?' While we were exchanging our tales and were locked in combat over which of us loved one or other of you more, a gong rang, signifying that my father had passed across to have his bath. And so after bathing in the wine-cellar we had dinner—I don't mean bathing in the cellar, but we did have dinner after bathing. We had fun listening to the country folk jeering at one another. After that back home, and before settling down to snore, I am unravelling my day's task and rendering an account of my day to my sweetest of masters; if I could long for you more, I would willingly be still further consumed.

The best of health to you, my Fronto, wheresoever you are, my honey-sweetest, my beloved, my delight. How are things between you and me? I adore you, absent though you are.

9 p. 71. Date uncertain. Fronto to Marcus, and reply.

If you love me at all, please sleep during those nights, that you may enter the senate with a healthy colour and read your speech sound of wind and limb.

To my master.

I shall never love you enough; I shall sleep.

10 pp. 71–2. Date uncertain. Fronto to Marcus, and reply.

To my lord.

Have pity on me, and remove one word from your speech; I entreat you never to use the word *dictio* (utterance) when you mean oration.

Farewell, my lord, my immortal glory. Please give my greetings to your lady mother.

To my master.

I shall tomorrow offer my defence of that word, if you remind me.

11 p. 74. Between 139 and 153. Marcus to Fronto, and reply.

To my master.

Such a time I have had of it these last few days! First my sister was suddenly seized by discomfort in her private parts, which made it painful to look at her. Then my mother hurt a rib against the corner of a wall, moving carelessly as she was so concerned about my sister; her injury seriously distressed both her and us. When I myself was going to retire, I found a scorpion in my bed! I made haste to kill it before I could lie down on top of it. If your own health is improved, that is a comfort. My mother is now in less severe condition, thanks be to the gods.

Fare well, best and sweetest master. My lady mother greets you.

To my lord.

I thank the gods with all my heart that they have you safe and uninjured. When I think back on your training. I feel confident that you are not disturbed; but as for me, however much you philosophic types may mock me, I was distraught!

Fare well, sweetest lord, and may heaven watch over you. Greet your lady mother from me.

12 pp. 47–9. Date uncertain, but before Marcus became emperor. Fronto to Marcus.

Fronto to my lord.

. . . would be softened, and so would find their way to the thoughts of the listener more effectively and without giving any offence. These are certainly what you think indirect and insincere devices, troublesome and ill suited to true friendship. But my own view is that without these arts, all rhetoric is laughable, boorish, untried, in a word without force and futile. Nor, I think, do philosophers have any less need of techniques of this sort than orators. In pleading this case I shall not call on witnesses of my own household, as they say, but on the most distinguished philosophers, the eldest and most illustrious poets, and finally the custom and civilized practice of everyday life, and what one finds to be the case with all the arts.

What, then, do you think of the famous Socrates, at once the leading light of both wisdom and eloquence? I have brought him forward first and foremost to give evidence before you. Did he use the style of speech you favour, in which there is nothing indirect, nothing occasionally deceptive? By what means did he manipulate and entrap Protagoras, Polus, Thrasymachus, and the rest of the sophists? And when did he ever encounter them straightforwardly? When did he not assail them from an ambush? Who was the man who gave birth to that upside-down oratory which the Greeks call irony? In what style did he generally approach and address Alcibiades and the rest of those young men who took such pride in their rank and beauty and means? Abusively, or with a more polished manner? By a fierce onslaught on their disgraceful doings, or by gentle argument? And Socrates certainly did not lack severity and forcefulness as great as that of the Cynic Diogenes with his ravings;* but he surely saw that the minds of mankind in general and young men in particular are more easily soothed by a cheerful and amiable speech than conquered by a vicious and aggressive one. Consequently he did not wage war against the misdeeds of the young using battering-rams or protective covering, but undermined them using secret passages; his audience never departed from his company torn and bleeding, but they sometimes left with a sense of having been challenged. For mankind is naturally reluctant to give way to those who attack, whereas we are amenable to those who coax and persuade us; so it is that we are readier to yield to those who plead with us than to be swayed by assailants, and advise stimulates us to mend our ways more effectively than abuse. Thus we fall in with the kindness of the adviser, but fight back against the harshness of the abuser.

13 p. 36.   150s AD.   Marcus to Fronto, and reply.

Aurelius Caesar to his dear Fronto, greeting.

I know you have often said to me that you wanted to know what you could do to please me most. The day has now arrived: now you can increase the strength of the love I feel for you (if it really can be increased). Not far away is that trial, the one in which men will be able not only to hear with goodwill your oratory, but also to witness with ill will your anger. I cannot see anyone who would dare to give you a word of advice in this matter. For those who are less your friends prefer to enjoy the sight of you pleading your case without any restraint; while those who are more your friends are afraid of seeming too well-disposed to your opponent if the deflect you from the natural course you would follow in prosecuting him. Furthermore, they cannot bear the thought of any particularly neat expression, that you have conceived with this case in mind, being denied you if you hold your peace. And so, whether you regard me as an impertinent adviser or a bold adolescent or as one who is too kindly disposed to your adversary, I shan't be slower on that account in offering advice which I do think conveys the better course. But why am I saying 'advice'? I am asking this of you, and asking it in the strongest terms, and I declare that if I do obtain this favour, I shall be in your debt. You'll say: 'What? If I'm attacked, am I not to pay him back in the same coin?' But you gain greater prestige at his expense if you refrain from replying at all when you have been attacked. But if he should do so first, certainly you can be pardoned for answering: I have asked him not to take the initiative himself, and I believe I have obtained his assurance. I am devoted to both of you, each according to his deserts, and I am conscious that he was actually educated in the household of my grandfather, Publius Calvisius, while I was educated with you. For these reasons I feel the greatest possible concern that this very distasteful business should be carried through as decently as possible.

I do hope that you will approve of my advice, for you certainly will approve of the wish that lies behind it. While I may be showing less sense in writing to you, I greatly prefer that fault to showing myself less your friend by remaining silent. Fare well, my dearest Fronto, best of friends.

Fronto to my lord Caesar.

It is with good cause that I have devoted myself to you, with good cause have I committed to you and your father the fruits of a lifetime's toil. What could be more friendly, more pleasant, more genuine than your letter? I beg you, no more of this talk of 'bold adolescent' or 'impertinent adviser'. Obviously, there is no danger that you would ever give youthful or ill-considered advice. Believe me, if you will (if not, I'll believe myself at any rate), your good sense exceeds that of your elders.

As for this affair, I feel conscious that your advice is sage and grey-haired, whereas my views are childish. For why should I provide a spectacle for the entertainment of fair and unfair observers? If this Herodes is a man of prudent and virtuous character, then it is not proper that such a man should be assailed by my invective; if, on the other hand, he is a good-for-nothing and a villain, then our conflict is not fought on equal terms, nor does he sustain as much harm as I do from it. For all association with a guilty man does harm to one's reputation, even if one wins. But I am sure that the former is the true situation: a man whom you judge worthy of your protection is surely an honest man. If I had ever realized this was your position, then may the gods bring me every misfortune, if I would ever have ventured to harm any friend of yours. Now I would ask you to help me in this area too with your advice, for the sake of the love you feel towards me, in which I am most blessed. I do not doubt that I should say nothing that might harm Herodes if it is extraneous to the case. But how to deal with those aspects which do fall within the case (and those are the most appalling)? That is what I am unsure of, and that is where I seek your advice. I am obliged to speak of free men savagely beaten and robbed, one of them even killed; I must speak of a disloyal son who spurned his father's prayers; I must denounce brutality and avarice; in this case Herodes must be set in the dock as a murderer. But if you think that I ought to use all my resources to attack my opponent and press him hard where the accusations on which the case rests are concerned, then please, best and sweetest lord, make me clearer in my mind about your advice. If, on the other hand, you think that I should hold myself back a little even with these charges, then I shall accept your wishes as the best course. As I have said, you can take it as firmly fixed and established that I shall say nothing about his character and the rest of his life that is not relevant to the case. But if you consider that I should obey the demands of the case, I warn you now that I shall not be making at all an unjustified use of the chance this case offers; for the charges involved are fierce and they must be fiercely presented. Those same points I mentioned (the cases of injury and brigandage) will be expressed by me in such language that they will be able to taste bile and venom; when I call him a miserable little Greek and an ignoramus, it will not be fatal.

Fare well, Caesar, and love me deeply, as you do now. But I also love the way you write your little letters, and so I wish that whenever you write me a line, you would use your own hand.

(Postscript). Hail, my lord.

My earlier letter was already closed and sealed when it occurred to me that it is possible that others who are also acting in this case (a great many advocates seem likely to be involved) may speak against Herodes with less restraint; please don't regard me as the one and only person responsible.

Fare well master, and live well, so that I may be happy. Capreolus, who is away at the moment, will be acting for the prosecution, and my friend Marcianus, and probably also Villianus.

14 pp. 65–8. Soon after Nov. 147. Marcus to Fronto, and reply.

Caesar to Fronto.

If the gods are on our side we seem to have some hope of safety: the bowels have dried up, the little fevers are over; but there is still a dreadful thinness and some slight coughing continues. You of course understand that I am writing to you about our darling little Faustina, for whom we have been working all out. Make sure that I know whether your state of health is in accordance with my prayers, dear master.

Fronto to Caesar.

Heavens above, how upset I was when I read the opening words of your letter! Because it was written so that I supposed that you were referring to some peril to your own health. Then once you'd revealed that the danger I'd taken to be your own from that opening was actually your daughter Faustina's, what an immense alteration in my panicky state of mind ensued! Not only an alteration, but I even somehow experienced some feeling of relief. You may well reply; 'What? Did a threat to my daughter's life seem less serious to you than a threat to my own? To you, who are always declaring that Faustina is to you what clear light is, or a feast-day, or hope close at hand, a prayer fulfilled, an unsullied joy, noble and undiluted renown?' For my part, I know what I experienced when I read your letter; but what the reason was for my feelings I cannot tell; I cannot tell why I was more distressed by the thought of yourself in danger than your daughter, unless perhaps, even if two pieces of news are equally grave, the one which the ears receive sooner carries more weight.

What the rationale behind such a phenomenon is, you should understand more readily than I, as you have some fuller knowledge of human nature and the feelings, and have learned such doctrines better than I have. I was trained to a moderate level of ability by my master—almost my father—Athenodotus, in the art of conceiving and adapting to the mind certain examples and images—semblances, he used to call them—and through this art I fancy I have found an image to explain why my fear seemed less severe when transferred to another person. The same thing generally does happen with people who are transporting a very heavy weight on their shoulders; when they shift their burden from the right shoulder to the left, even though there is no reduction in the weight, nevertheless it is felt to be both a shifting and an alleviation of the load.

Now, since in the latter part of your letter, in which you reported that Faustina was now a tiny bit better, you disposed of all my panic and anxiety, this does not seem an inappropriate moment to speak more freely and openly about my love for you. After all, those who have just been released from great fear and distress are generally permitted some degree of frivolity and foolishness. I am aware of the depth of my love for you from many childish tests as well as from serious and weighty evidence. I shall give you some idea now of the nature of these childish proofs.

If I ever see you in my dreams, when (as the poet says)* 'I am chained by soft and peaceful slumber', I invariably rush to embrace you and cover you with kisses. Then according to the 'plot' of each dream, I either weep copiously or rejoice out of happiness or pleasure. This is one proof of my love, drawn from the *Annals* [of Ennius], a poetical and rather a sleepy-headed proof.

Have another, this one an argumentative and critical proof. There have been times when I have complained about you to my innermost circle of friends in quite severe terms, when you yourself were not present. Occasionally, for example, this happened when you entered a gathering more solemnly than you should; or when you would read books at the games or at a dinner-party (in those days I myself was not yet too old for the games and parties). On such occasions I used to call you a dour fellow, one who did not observe the proper time and place for such behaviour, sometimes, provoked by anger, I even called you objectionable. But if anybody else started disparaging you in the same style in my hearing, I couldn't listen without losing my temper. You see, it was easier for me to talk that way myself than to put up with other people speaking ill of you, just as I would be readier to strike my darling daughter Gratia myself than to tolerate anybody else doing so.

A third item for me to add from my foolish proofs. You know how all the money-changers, small-scale banks, shops, inns, roof-eaves, porches, window-frames, practically anywhere you look, all have your portrait set up on view, most of them badly done, I agree, and made or sculpted with the aid of a dull Minerva, even a Minerva of clay. But whenever your portrait catches my eyes on my promenade, however unlike its original model, it never fails to make my lips pucker up for a kiss, or to make me dream of you. [The text here is very far from certain.]

And now, putting a halt to my foolishness, let me turn to serious matters. This letter of yours in particular has shown me how greatly I love you, when I was more alarmed by the thought of you in danger than of your daughter. Otherwise, at other times, I want you to be safe as much as myself, your daughter as much as you, as is only right. But see here! you must make sure not to play the informer and appear to give evidence before your daughter that I care for you more than I do for her. For there is a danger that your daughter, distressed by this news, may grow angry (for she's a stern lady, after the ancient pattern), and when I ask to kiss her hands and feet she might withdraw them or stretch them out more reluctantly because of this grudge; and by the gods, I would rather bestow my kisses on those sweet little hands and those fat little feet than on your imperial neck or your virtuous and pleasant face!

15 pp. 109–10. Between AD 161 and 167; M. is now emperor. Fronto to Marcus.

Fronto to my lord Antoninus Augustus.

I think I may well be considered the most eloquent of mankind ever born and endowed with the gift of speech, now that you, Marcus Aurelius, take the trouble to read my works and approve them and amidst such heavy duties do not regard the spending of your precious hours even on my orations as time spent without profit or advantage.

If it is because of your love for me that you find pleasure in my talents, then I am the most fortunate of mankind, because I am so high in your affections that I even seem to you a gifted speaker; if, on the other hand, this is your real opinion, and you make this judgement with a critical eye and after reflection, then I shall feel justified in thinking myself a fine speaker, since I seem so to you.

But I am not greatly surprised that you read with pleasure the eulogies of your father which I delivered in the senate when I was consul-designate and entered upon my office; for you could listen even to Parthians and Spaniards praising your father in their native tongues and still take them for the greatest orators who ever lived. It was not my speech, but your father's fine qualities that you admired; you praised not the words of the praise-singer, but the achievements of the man praised.

As for your own eulogy, which I produced in the senate on the same day, what I would like you to feel about that is as follows:

that in those days, you showed the highest potential, whereas now we see in you supreme virtue. Then, the corn was burgeoning in the field, while now the harvest is complete and the crop is stored in the barn. I had hopes then, I now have the reality; hope becomes fact.

[The remainder of the letter exists only in disjointed fragments.]

16 pp. 131–3 (badly damaged and only recoverable in extracts). After 161. Fronto to Marcus.

Fronto to Antoninus Augustus.

. . . Moreover, who can fail to be aware that among the poets Lucilius is subtle, Albucius dry, Lucretius sublime, Pacuvius second-rate, Accius uneven, Ennius diverse? As for history, similarly Sallust wrote methodically, Pictor disjointedly, Claudius elegantly, Antias tastelessly, Sisenna long-windedly, Cato in long chain-gangs of words, Coelius one word at a time. In public speeches, Cato spoke violently, Gracchus all in a flood, Cicero amply. Again, in forensic oratory the same Cato rages, whereas Cicero exults, Gracchus rants, Calvus quarrels.

But you may perhaps have little time for examples such as these. What about the philosophers? Didn't they use different styles of speaking? Zeno is superbly clear in exposition, Socrates is the expert in finding fault and refutation, Diogenes is the readiest to turn to abuse, Heraclitus wraps everything in obscurity, Pythagoras has an amazing way of giving dignity to everything by use of secret symbols, while Clitomachus is two-faced and calls everything into question. What then would these thinkers, the very wisest of men, have achieved if they were all deprived of their own ways and their training? If Socrates was prevented from refuting people, Zeno from making distinctions, Diogenes from attacking? If Pythagoras wasn't allowed to give anything sacred status, Heraclitus was barred from concealing anything, Clitomachus from finding anything ambiguous?

But I should try not to spend longer on this first part of the argument than the bounds of a letter require. Time then to consider your own views on words. My dear fellow, do tell me whether you think that I should scorn and reject a more elegant formulation, even though it may come into my mind spontaneously, without any effort or any concentration on my part? Or do you bar me from finding elegant wording by effort and attention, while ordering me to allow them admittance if they turn up unbidden and uninvited, like Menelaus at the feast?* For that prohibition is surely a harsh one and inhumane; it's just as if you were to refuse a host's offer of a glass of Falernian (which is native to his district and so he has a plentiful supply) and demand that he provide you with Cretan or Saguntian,* which he would have to go asking for elsewhere, and purchase it specially.

. . . What of Euphrates, Dio, Timocrates, Athenodotus, men whom we ourselves remember? What about Musonius, who taught them? Were they not endowed with exceptional rhetorical skills? Didn't they become no less famous for their distinguished oratory than for their wisdom? Or do you . . .

. . . he would not have preferred a stained and filthy cloak to a smart white one that had been properly washed. Or perhaps you think that he [Epictetus] deliberately became lame or was born a slave on purpose? Well then, what *is* it? . . .

[The rest of the letter is lost; no doubt there was more in the same vein. It is a theme to which Fronto often returns; cf. ii. 52–84 Haines.]

17 pp. 220–3. Late AD 164/early 165. Marcus to Fronto, and reply.

Marcus to Fronto.

Greetings to my master. I just learned of your loss. As I am tormented whenever you suffer pain in your limbs, what do you suppose my feelings are when it is your heart that feels the pain? In my distress, nothing else comes to mind for me to say but to ask you for my sake to preserve yourself, my sweetest master, in whom I find more comfort in this life than you can find for this sad loss from any source.

I did not write this in my own hand, as even my hand was trembling after my evening bath. My most delightful of masters, fare well.

Fronto to Antoninus Augustus.*

Through all my life fortune has pursued me with sorrows of this kind. For, leaving out my other bitter experiences, I have lost five of my children and the timing of my losses has been particularly wretched, since in each and every case the child I lost was my only one. I have suffered such a series of bereavements that I have only ever had a son when I had lost one. So it is that always when I lost children I have been denied any comfort from those who were left behind; fatherhood and recent grief went together.

But I bore more courageously those sorrows by which I alone was tortured. For my mind met my grief head-on, and resisted it on equal terms, like one man matched against another in single combat. But now, with the loss of my grandson, my own grief is multiplied by the grief of my daughter, the grief of my son-in-law. I endured my own distress, I cannot bear the grief of my own. I waste away and dissolve in tears together with my beloved Victorinus.

Many a time I demand an explanation from the immortal gods, I accuse and abuse the fates. Was this fair and right in any way, that Victorinus, a man of the utmost devoutness, gentleness, truthfulness, and morality, an exceptionally civilized man, should be struck down by the death of his son, such a miserable blow? If the world is governed by providence, was this justly foreseen and planned? If all human life is decreed by destiny, was destiny obliged to decree this? Is there then no distinction between the fates of good and bad men? Do the gods, the fates, have no way of deciding formally what kind of man is to be robbed of his son? A human being steeped in crime and evil-doing, who had better never have been born, sometimes brings up his children safe and sound, and when he dies they survive him. But Victorinus, a man of saintly virtue, the kind of man the country needs in as large numbers as possible, has been deprived of his beloved son. Damn it, what kind of providence has such bad eyesight? They say the Fates are so called from *fari* (to utter): is this the right kind of utterance for them to make? The poets give the Fates a distaff and the threads of life to spin; but certainly no wool-spinner is so useless and ignorant as to use a tough and knotted thread for the master's toga and a fine and subtle strand for the slave's. If good men are struck down by grief, while bad men can prosper and enjoy their homes and families, I regard that sample of the Fates' spinning as measured and weighed all wrong.

It may be, however, that I am in the grip of a different kind of delusion; perhaps in my ignorance of the true state of things I long for what is evil as if it were beneficial, while I shrink from what is good thinking it to be ill, and perhaps death itself, which all men think a cause for grief, in fact brings an end to suffering and cares and disasters and transports us, freed from the unhappy bondage of the body, to the regions of peace and delight, a place full of all good things, the place where the souls meet and mingle together. That I could more easily credit than that all human life is governed by an evil providence, or by none at all.

But if, by this argument, it is in fact the case that death is a matter for congratulation, not lamentation, then the younger anyone attains that blessing, the happier he must be considered, and the more welcome in the divine company; the younger one dies, the sooner one is freed from the ills of the body, the sooner one is summoned forth to assume the glorious state of a free soul. Yet this may well be true, but it is of little concern to us, who are longing for those whom we have lost; nor does the immortality of souls console us when we, for as long as we live, are deprived of our nearest and dearest. We miss the familiar stance, the voice, the form, we grieve over the pitiful looks of those who have passed on, the lips closed, the eyes upturned, the colour departed from every part of the body. However universal the agreement that souls are immortal, this will remain an argument for philosophic disquisition, not a cure for parental longing.

However these things are organized from on high, they certainly will not distress me for any great length of time, since my own death is so near at hand. Whether we are forever extinguished, (as?) I at one time desired . . .

[There is a gap in the text here, in which only scattered words are legible.]

And now my darling grandson, whom I myself am bringing up in my heart, he is the one who tears my being and tortures me more and more as time goes on. For in the image I have of him I look on the one who was lost, I picture his face, I imagine the sound of a voice that fits the boy's mind. My grief creates the illusion and contemplates it; as I do not know the true appearance of the dead boy, I am tormented as I grasp at plausible notions.

My daughter will show her wisdom. She will find relief in her husband, as good a man as the race can produce; he will console her with tears when she weeps, with sighs when she sighs, speaking when she does, being silent when she is. I, her ancient father, am not a suitable comforter: it would have been more fitting for me to have died before him. None of the songs of the poets, no teachings of philosophers, can be as effective in soothing my daughter's grief and softening her pain, as the voice of her husband, emanating from the fondest of lips, from the heart that is closest to her own.

As for me, my comfort will be my age, already almost spent and close now to death. When that end comes, whether the hour be night or day, in the moment of departure I shall extend my greetings to heaven and declare what I know to be the case: that in a long life I have done nothing which could be judged disgraceful or wicked or criminal; that in the course of my life there has been no offence of mine involving avarice or treachery; that, on the contrary, I have performed many generous deeds, many out of friendship, many out of loyalty, many with resolution, and often even at the risk of my own life.

With my excellent brother I lived on the best of terms, and rejoiced at his achievement of the highest office through the generosity of your father, while now I see him in a peaceful and amply secure condition thanks to your friendship. As for the distinctions that I myself have obtained, I never sought them for improper motives. I have devoted more pains to the improvement of my mind than my body. I put the pursuit of learning ahead of any concern for property. I preferred to be a poor man rather than dependent on others' aid, to be in need rather than to be demanding help. I was never extravagant, though I sometimes had to undertake necessary expenditure. I told the truth diligently, I listened to the truth willingly. I thought it better to be ignored than to be flattered, better to keep silent than to fabricate, better to be a friend in season than a hanger-on at all seasons. I sought little, but my deserts were not so little. I obliged everyone as far as was in my power, that is, as best I could. I gave assistance more readily to the deserving, more boldly to the undeserving. If a man showed no gratitude, that did not make me less keen to do him what good I could promptly. Nor was I ever at all unpleasant to the unappreciative.

[The rest of the letter, amounting to perhaps one more paragraph, is illegible.]

EXPLANATORY NOTES

The *Meditations*

Book I

On the special character of the first book, see Introduction, pp. xv–xvi.

1 *From . . .*: throughout the book Marcus omits the verb which the sense requires. Some translators insert, e.g. 'I learned' or 'I acquired', but this is wrong, for many of these qualities are such that Marcus would not claim to possess them. This is made explicit in i. 17 ('though I still come somewhat short of this by my own fault'). It is in fact difficult to find a verb that will suit every instance. A paraphrase such as 'I am grateful to X for' might be more satisfactory.

grandfather: M. Annius Verus, consul of AD 97, 121, and 126, a distinguished figure who was the first of the line to gain patrician status. He died in 138. After his father's death Marcus was adopted by his grandfather. See further Birley, *Marcus Aurelius*, ch. 2.

2 *memory of him*: Marcus' father, also called M. Annius Verus in the common Roman fashion, died when his son was a mere boy, probably in 124.

3 *mother*: Domitia Lucilla, a wealthy and cultivated lady, frequently mentioned in the correspondence with Fronto; some of his letters to her are preserved. Her importance in Marcus' life after his father's death will be obvious.

4 *mother's grandfather*: L. Catilius Severus (Birley, pp. 33, 36).

good teachers at home: this was the traditional Roman practice, but by no means always followed in this period: see the complaints of Tacitus, *Dialogue on Orators*, 28-9, and the advice of Quintilian, *The Education of an Orator*, i. 1. See further S. F. Bonner, *Education in Ancient Rome* (Methuen, London, 1977).

5 *tutor*: oddly unnamed, perhaps a slave as opposed to the learned scholars and statesmen mentioned later.

races . . . gladiators: barred from sensible men's conversation by Epictetus, *Handbook*, xxxiii. 2.

6 *Diognetus*: according to the *Historia Augusta*, Marcus' painting instructor.

sorcerers, incantations, exorcism: all of these were well-known phenomena in the pagan world (hence there is no need to connect this sentence with Christianity, as some have done): see Lucian, *Lovers of Lies*, for an amusing satire on the kind of stories current. In general see R. MacMullen, *Enemies of the Roman Order* (Cambridge Mass. and London, 1966), chs. 3 and 4.

cock-fight: a slight mistranslation; it should be 'quail-fight'.

Baccheius: a Platonic philosopher of the day; the others are unknown.

7 *Rusticus*: one of the three men Marcus was most grateful to have known (i. 17 below), and one of his most interesting mentors. Q. Iunius Rusticus, consul in 162 for the second time, was the most influential figure in arousing Marcus' interest in philosophy, and perhaps especially in Stoicism: there are traces in the Fronto correspondence of some degree of rivalry between the two disciplines, and their advocates, for Marcus' attention. Rusticus' interest in philosophy may be partly attributed to his descent from one of the Stoic aristocrats martyred in the name of liberty and opposition to tyranny under Domitian (Q. Arulenus Iunius Rusticus, condemned in AD 93). See MacMullen (cited in last note), ch. 1.

to be easily recalled to myself: this phrase should be linked with i. 17, 'that though I was often angry with Rusticus I never went to extremes for which I should have been sorry'. In general, anger and its suppression is a recurrent topic in the *Meditations*: see esp. xi. 18.

Epictetus: a freed slave turned Stoic teacher and lecturer. Exiled by Domitian, he continued teaching in Nicopolis. He is the most important stylistic and ethical influence on Marcus, who often quotes or imitates him. This and other references are not to books by Epictetus himself (as far as we know he wrote nothing), but to the compilation by his disciple Arrian (also the author of historical and other works). Eight books of moral discourses were known to the ancient world, of which four survive.

8 *Apollonius*: of Chalcedon, Stoic philosopher and 'sophist' (i.e. wealthy professional orator and teacher). Some held him in less esteem than Marcus, who counts him as one of the three men he is most grateful to have known (i. 17). Contrast Lucian, *Demonax*, 31; *Augustan History: Life of Pius*, x. 4.

9 *Sextus*: of Chaeronea in Boeotia, a relation (probably nephew) of the gifted biographer and philosopher Plutarch. Even in his old age Marcus continued to attend Sextus' lectures (Philostratus, *Lives of the Sophists*, II. i. 557).

10 *Alexander the grammarian*: of Cotiaeum in Syria. An eminent literary figure of the Greek world and a leading authority on Homer. He also taught the great sophist Aelius Aristides, who composed a funeral oration (still extant) in his memory.

11 *Fronto*: because of the survival of some of the correspondence between Cornelius Fronto and Marcus (and others of his family), we know him more vividly than any of the other people mentioned in the Meditations: see the extracts translated in the Appendix. He was Marcus' tutor in rhetoric, but like most of his teachers remained a friend

well after his pupil became emperor. He probably died *c.* AD 167. Striking here is the fact that Marcus says nothing at all about Fronto's formal training in style and language, but concentrates on the moral debt.

The second point Marcus makes here can be connected with two passages in Fronto's letters. In one (i. 280 H.) Marcus' teacher remarks that the Romans lack a word for 'natural affection', using the Greek word *philostorgos*, the negative form of which Marcus uses here. In the other, writing to Verus to recommend a friend, Fronto describes his friend as having 'a sense of honour patently Roman, a warmth of affection, however, that is perhaps not Roman, for there is nothing I have found less often at Rome in all my life than a man sincerely affectionate (*philostorgon*)' (ii. 154). Clearly this was a regular topic with Fronto (who was himself a 'new man', an outsider from Cirta in Roman Africa).

12 *Alexander the Platonist*: a philosopher-orator from Seleucia in Cilicia. It is relevant that he was probably serving by now as Marcus' Greek secretary.

F. Millar, in his massive study *The Emperor in the Roman World* (Duckworth, London, 1977), documents the burden of an emperor's administrative labour. He begins with a striking anecdote (told of Hadrian and several other monarchs) in which a woman pursues a ruler with a petition. He pleads that he has no time to read it, whereupon she calls out after him 'Then stop being a king!' (references in Millar, p. 3).

13 *Catulus*: Cinna Catulus, another Roman figure, but otherwise little known. The *Historia Augusta* calls him a Stoic.

Athenodotus: a Stoic who was also a former tutor of Fronto (i. 204, 270; ii. 50 H). *Domitius* is unidentified; there is presumably a story, lost to us, connecting them as teacher and pupil.

14 *Severus*: Cnaeus Claudius Severus Arabianus, consul 146; his son (consul II 173) married Marcus' eldest daughter.

Thrasea, Helvidius, Cato, Dio, Brutus: an unchronological array of famous figures who suffered as a result of their efforts to bring philosophic principle into the practice of politics. Thrasea Paetus was a senator of the reign of Nero, a Stoic, and by the end of his career an enemy of the emperor. He was forced to kill himself in AD 66. The elder Helvidius Priscus, Thrasea's son-in-law, was executed under Vespasian (AD 74); the younger Helvidius was executed in a similar purge by Domitian (AD 93). Cato the younger, the last serious opponent of Julius Caesar, killed himself once it became clear that the Republican cause was doomed in the Civil Wars (46 BC); his death was long remembered and valued as an example by opponents of tyranny under the Empire. Brutus, Cato's son-in-law, was of course the assassin of Julius Caesar (44 BC); he was later defeated by Octavian and Antony, and killed himself at the battle of Philippi (42 BC). The identity of Dio is less clear. Marcus probably means the Syracusan aristocrat who, inspired by Plato's teaching, tried to make the tyrant Dionysius II into a philosopher king, a project which ended in messy failure (Plutarch pairs Dio and Brutus in his *Parallel Lives*). The other possibility, that the reference is to Dio of Prusa (Dio Chrysostom or 'Golden-mouthed'), a sophist of recent times exiled by Domitian, seems much less likely.

the idea of a commonwealth . . .: the language here echoes theoretical writings by Stoics and others on ideal kingship. Marcus means that through his instruction in the history of the Stoic opposition Severus led him to understand the need for a better kind of monarchy, an ideal he has tried to fulfil.

15 *Maximus*: Claudius Maximus, consul of *c.* 142. Also mentioned at the end of i. 16 and in i. 17 as one of the three men Marcus is glad to have known. He was military governor of Pannonia (AD 150–4) and proconsul of Africa (158), where he presided over the trial of Apuleius, sophist and novelist,

charged with magical practices: see Apuleius' surviving defence speech, the *Apology*, which pays flattering tribute to Maximus' learning and philosophic wisdom. He seems to have been a Stoic. He was dead by the time Marcus wrote vii. 25.

16 By far the longest portrait, this chapter recounts Marcus' debts to his adoptive father, the emperor Antoninus Pius (reigned from 10 July 138 to 7 March 161). The past tenses used throughout strongly suggest that he is dead (as is explicit in the parallel ch. vi. 30).

unnatural practices: one of Farquharson's more prudish renderings. More exact would be 'love of boys'. Roman traditionalism frowned on homosexuality, though in fact it was widely practised even in the highest circles.

his manner of life . . . of this sort: the allusions are obscure to us, but obviously clear memories for Marcus.

Socrates: the famous Athenian thinker (d. 399 BC), who was renowned for his self-discipline. In Plato's *Symposium* it is remarked that no one could ever outdrink Socrates or get him drunk (176c, 220a).

Maximus: see ch. 15 above, where again his endurance of illness is singled out.

17 *second wife*: more correctly, 'concubine'; but his grandfather only took a mistress when his legal wife had died.

not to need . . . pomp: the historians who provide narrative accounts of Marcus' reign also refer to his simplicity of dress and way of life.

brother: his adoptive brother and co-emperor Lucius Verus, who died in 169. He had the reputation of being a playboy, but some of the evidence is merely gossip, and there was a natural tendency for ancient (and modern) writers to play up the contrast between him and the serious Marcus.

life in obedience to Nature: this was the Stoic ideal: see Introduction, p. xii.

the gods . . . inspirations: this passage is decisive evidence that Marcus believed he had had some kind of religious experience, but it is hard to say more. The reference to dreams later in this chapter gives a further clue. See also ix. 27, 40; fuller discussion in my *The Meditations of Marcus Aurelius*, ch. 5.

Benedicta and Theodotus: almost certainly slaves of the imperial household; otherwise unknown. Note again the mixture of candour and allusiveness in sexual matters.

my wife: Faustina, whom Marcus married in 145. She died in 175, much to Marcus' distress. The present tense used here perhaps suggests that she was still alive when this pasage was written. Scandal did not spare her, but Marcus' own words should caution us against believing the tales of her infidelities.

dreams: a common source of supernatural guidance in antiquity, discussed at length by Cicero in *On Divination*. See R. Lane Fox, *Pagans and Christians*, 150–67.

the answer . . . thyself: the text here is badly corrupt, and the reference to an oracle is quite uncertain. Even if we were sure what Marcus actually wrote, it looks like another opaque allusion.

although . . . in the clouds: Marcus contrasts the ethical concerns which for him are the true task of philosophy with the idle speculations or frivolous pastimes of some intellectuals who might call themselves 'philosophers' or 'sophists' (the borderline was often blurred).

the gods . . . hand: the rhythm suggests that this phrase is a quotation, but the source is unknown.

Book II

Written among the Quadi, on the river Gran: the Gran is a tributary of the Danube. Cf. the heading to book iii, 'written at Carnuntum'. Only books ii and iii have such headings. This seems a sign that they are authentic: a forger would probably have inserted these geographical entries throughout. At least part of the *Meditations* was therefore composed on campaign; Carnuntum lies slightly south of the border between free Germany and the Roman province of Pannonia, and the Quadi were among the tribes Marcus made war upon during the 170s. (The exact chronology is obscure in the absence of a full and reliable military narrative.) See A. Birley, *Marcus Aurelius*, ch. 8.

1 *in the early morning*: cf. v. 1.

ignorance: Stoics followed the intellectual conception of virtue as knowledge of good and evil, associated earlier with Plato's Socrates. If a man knows and truly understands the nature of wrongdoing, he will not commit wrong. Christian doctrines of original sin and modern psychology make this view harder for us to accept.

a portion of divinity: a very frequent idea in the *Meditations* and other Stoic writings: man's true being is his governing self, the mind or soul, which is identical to or partakes of the nature of God. Since Stoicism was a materialist philosophy, this is to be understood in a literal and not a metaphorical sense. Cf. ii. 4 'from whom you subsist as an effluence'; ii. 13; iii. 5.

2 *You are an old man*: born in 121, Marcus was 59 when he died, and the *Meditations* are probably all the product of his last decade. For his old age see ii. 6; v. 31; x. 15; xii. 1.

3 *that other world*: cf. ii. 17. This is more like Platonism (which envisages a more real and divine world on a different plane from ours) than Stoicism. On Marcus' 'otherworldliness' see the fine remarks by E. R. Dodds, *Pagan and Christian in an Age of Anxiety*, 5–14, 20–2. For animosity to the physical, see vi. 13; viii. 24 (with n.), etc.

put away your thirst for books: cf. ii. 2, 'put away your books'; iii. 14; viii. 3, 'you are not able to read . . .'

6 *violence*: that is, spiritual harm. For elucidation of the nature of this harm see esp. ii. 16.

commit your well-being to the charge of other men's souls: by paying attention to their opinions, especially whether they praise or blame him. Indifference to others' (misguided or ill-informed) views is a lesson that Marcus constantly tries to learn: cf. ii. 11, 12; iv. 6, 20; vi. 16, and often.

10 *Theophrastus*: one of the great disciples of Aristotle, succeeding him in 322 BC as head of his school. Many of his works are lost, and this quotation (fr. 77 Wimmer) is from one such work.

11 *if gods exist*: not an expression of scepticism, but part of a process of reasoned argument. For Marcus' reflections on the gods and their activities and concerns, compare esp. i. 17; vi. 44; ix. 27, 40; xii. 5. He tends to speak in vaguely generalized terms of 'the gods' or Nature' or 'the Universe': the terms are virtually synonymous. There is little sign that he thought of the traditional Olympian deities as individual entities with the personalities they possess in myth and poetry. In general for Roman intellectuals' thinking about the gods and providence see Cicero's absorbing dialogue *On the Nature of the Gods* (available in the Loeb series); book ii presents Stoic ideas, and in book iii these are criticized.

13 *as Pindar says*: the Greek does not actually give the name of the source, but simply 'he says'. Perhaps Marcus had momentarily forgotten the source? Greatest of the Greek lyric poets, Pindar flourished in the mid-fifth century BC. But the quotation (fr. 292 Snell) is a famous one, and Marcus may be thinking as much of its use in Plato (*Theaetetus*, 173e).

14 The themes of this chapter are close to those of the genre known as 'consolation', usually an essay or letter to one recently bereaved, pointing out the transience of human life and suggesting reasons for being reconciled to one's loss. Though such works often seem cold to us, they were extremely popular in the ancient world, especially at Rome: see e.g. Servius Sulpicius to Cicero, *Letters to his friends*, iv. 5; Horace, *Odes*, I. xxiv; Seneca, *Consolations* to Marcia,

Helvia, and Polybius. Marcus often draws on ideas of this kind (that life is the same whatever its length; that death is inevitable even for the great; that the time after death will be just like the time before we were born): for other chapters in this vein see iii. 3; iv. 32, 33, 48, 50; vi. 27, 47; vii. 49; viii. 5, 25, 31; x. 27, 34; xii. 27.

15 *the Cynic philosopher Monimus*: a figure of the fourth century BC. See Diogenes Laertius, *Lives of the Philosophers*, vi. 82–3; A. W. Gomme and F. H. Sandbach, *Menander: a Commentary* (Oxford, 1973), 696–7.

16 *a separate growth*: in the Stoic conception of the Universe all things are united, part of an ordered whole (iv. 34, 45; ix. 8; xii. 30); so too in their ethics, man is a social being with duties to other human beings. Cf. viii. 34, xi. 8.

the most venerable of all cities and government: Marcus refers not to the Roman empire or Rome itself (though he is far from indifferent to his status as a Roman: ii. 5; iii. 5, 14; vi. 44), but to the world, conceived as a greater city or cosmopolis, of which all living men are fellow-citizens. Cf. iii. 11; iv. 3, 4, 23, 29; x. 15; xii. 36. The idea is traditional in Stoicism: see e.g. Cicero, *On the Nature of the Gods*, i. 121; Epictetus, III. xxii. 4, 22, 47, 83; A. A. Long and D. Sedley, *The Hellenistic Philosophers*, i (Cambridge, 1987), 330, 332, 348, 429–37. It seems not, however, to involve social consequences or a commitment to political reform: see Epictetus, III. xiii. 9 ff.; H. C. Baldry, *The Unity of Mankind in Greek Thought* (Cambridge, 1965), 151–66.

17 *his life a warfare*: another traditional image: see v. 31 n.

from that other world: cf. ii. 3 n.

Book III

Carnuntum: see note on the heading at the start of book ii.

1 *whether the time is come to take leave of life*: Stoics advocated suicide when it was no longer possible to perform the duties of life. The Stoic fathers Zeno and Cleanthes had killed

themselves, and the heroic death of the younger Cato (cf. i. 14 n.) provided a precedent of a different kind. For suicide to escape a crippling or painful illness, compare Lucretius, iii. 1039 ff.; Seneca, *Letters*, xxx; lviii. 32 ff.; Pliny, *Letters*, i. 12. For Marcus on suicide see further v. 29; viii. 47; x. 22, 32.

2 For the thought, and some of the examples, cf. vi. 36.

3 *Hippocrates*: legendary founder of the medical art, still remembered for the Oath sworn by members of his profession.

Chaldean: i.e. Babylonian. The East and in particular Babylon was regarded as a source of astrological learning.

Heraclitus: Pre-Socratic thinker, *c.* 500 BC.

Vermin killed Democritus; another kind of vermin . . .: in the first case, lice; in the second, the ungrateful Athenian public who condemned Socrates to death in 399. The reference to Democritus seems to be a slip for Pherecydes: both are Pre-Socratic thinkers.

5 *a Roman*: cf. ii. 5; ii. 16 n.

you should stand upright: cf. vii. 12.

6 *as Socrates used to say*: the exact source is unclear, though the idea of withdrawal from sense-perceptions is reminiscent of Plato's *Phaedo*.

'*But the higher . . .*': here Marcus imagines an anonymous opponent responding to his argument. This is a regular technique in rhetoric and moral essays; it serves to make a contrasting view more vivid.

10 *little the corner of the earth he lives in . . .*: the minuteness of human life and the human world is a recurrent theme in the *Meditations*: cf. v. 24; vi. 36; vii. 48–9; viii. 21, etc.; E. R. Dodds, *Pagan and Christian in an Age of Anxiety*, 8.

11 *to see distinctly what it is in its essence, naked . . .*: this process of analysis leads to some startlingly reductive results: cf. esp. vi. 13, and the discussion in my *The* Meditations *of Marcus Aurelius: A Study*, ch. 4. iii.

13 *doctors*: the medical analogy for philosophy is an important clue to the purpose of the *Meditations*: see Introduction, p. xiv.

14 *notebooks . . . deeds . . . extracts*: suggestive for Marcus' literary tastes and practice. 'Deeds of ancient Rome and Greece' probably refers to a collection of notable examples from the past (cf. Valerius Maximus' nine books of *Memorable Deeds and Sayings*). We see some evidence of 'extracts' in the *Meditations* themselves, esp. at vii. 35 ff. For Marcus' reading and his didactic approach to literature see x. 34; xi. 6.

15 *They*: the *stúlti* ('fools'), those who do not grasp the truths that philosophy teaches.

16 *men who sin against nature*: the correct translation is 'pathics' or 'catamites'.

Phalaris: tyrant of Acragas (now Agrigento) in Sicily in the late sixth century BC. He was a byword for cruelty, and was said to have roasted his victims alive in a brazen bull.

men who do not believe in gods . . . locked their doors: this passage has sometimes been taken to refer to the Christians (see e.g. Haines, Loeb edition, pp. 63, 385–6), but this is quite unnecessary. See xi. 3 n.

Book IV

1 The idea here is that a man's reason can treat all external circumstances as raw material for its rational consideration; obstacles can be absorbed, i.e. treated with proper detachment and viewed through rational eyes. Cf. v. 20; vi. 50; perhaps viii. 41.

3 On 'withdrawal', physical and spiritual, see A. J. Festugière, *Personal Religion among the Greeks* (Berkeley and Los Angeles, 1954), 58 ff. Horace and other authors recommend withdrawal to a country retreat to escape the hubbub of civic life and politics (*Odes*, III, xxix, etc.); but moralists also regularly insist that it is the inner self, not

external circumstances, which must be adjusted: 'caelum non animum mutant qui trans mare currunt' ('those who dash across the sea change the skies above them, not their state of mind', Horace, *Epistles*, I. xi. 27; cf. Seneca, *Letters*, xxviii). Similarly, Marcus writes that he should find peace within himself: philosophy grants comfort and retreat, which no change of scene can provide.

brief and fundamental truths: brief because they will thus be more memorable. Brevity was acclaimed as a virtue in Stoic stylistics, and Marcus both recommends (iii. 5; v. 7; viii. 30) and practises it in the *Meditations*.

the alternative: 'either Providence or blind atoms': the first alternative is of course the Stoic view; the second refers to the Epicurean doctrine that life and the world came into being by the random combination of atoms. Elsewhere Marcus again uses 'atoms' as shorthand for Epicureanism: viii. 17; ix. 28, 39, etc.

citizen: cf. iii. 11; iv. 4.

6 *fig tree*: cf. viii. 15; xii. 16.

12 *the principle of the royal and law-giving art*: it is the art of ruling, not Marcus himself, that lays down the law. Note the concern for the good of his subjects: cf. i. 14; iii. 4 (opening).

if someone is there to correct: Marcus is willing to be shown he is wrong, by an adviser or subordinate. Cf. esp. v. 28 n.; viii. 16.

14 On the transience of human existence, cf. vii. 23, 25; viii. 50; xii. 23.

15 The analogy is between the grains of incense and human lives.

16 *those*: who are the judges whose views will be altered by Marcus' reformation? Perhaps the gods?

18 *who does not look to what his neighbour . . .*: cf. iii. 4.

a black character: cf. iv. 28.

19 Something has perhaps dropped out of the text at the end of this chapter.

21 *If souls continue to exist*: for Marcus' uncertainty on this point see esp. xii. 5; also iii. 3; vi. 24; vii. 32; viii. 25, 58.

23 The passage is one which comes close to Christian devotion and expression: cf. Paul, Romans 11: 36.

   dear city of Cecrops: the phrase is quoted from the comedian Aristophanes (fr. 112 Kassel–Austin). Cecrops was a mythical god-king of early Athens.

24 *Democritus*: see iii. 3 n. The saying is fr. B3 Diels–Kranz.

26 *the thread was spun*: the web of fate is a favourite image in Marcus for Providence's predetermined scheme. Cf. iii. 11; iv. 34.

27 *intermingled and sympathetic*: since all things were material and derived from the same elemental origins, Stoics commonly held that all parts of the cosmos were bound together in a sympathetic relationship, even when not physically connected. This idea was the basis of their belief in divination. Hence order in the soul must be mirrored by order in the structure of the Universe, and vice versa. 'Cosmos' itself, indeed, means 'order', a point which philosophers made play with: see Plato, *Gorgias*, 508a.

28 There is no word for 'is' in the Greek, and it should probably be deleted from the translation. Is this an outburst against an unnamed individual, or a list of abusive terms? This chapter is a mystery.

29 For the thought, cf. viii. 52. 'Foreigner', because all men belong to one cosmopolitan community, cf. ii. 16 n.; iv. 23. To ignore the obligations of membership of that community is to cut oneself out of society and the human race: cf. viii. 34; xi. 8. For related images, see v. 9; ix. 2; x. 32; Paul, 1 Thessalonians 5: 4 ff., Romans 13:11.

30 *Philosopher without a tunic*: probably a reference to the rough-living Cynics, the most famous of whom, Diogenes, lived in a barrel. Cf. Epictetus, III. xxii. 45 ff.

32 For the sequence of thought and the examples used, cf. 33, 48, 50; viii. 25. Vespasian was emperor from AD 69 to 79, Trajan from 98 to 117.

33 . . . *archaisms*: for the parallel between verbal usage and human lives compare Horace, *Ars Poetica*, 60–72.

Camillus . . . Dentatus: great men of the Roman republic. There were several famous Scipios, but the best known was Publius Cornelius Scipio Africanus, conqueror of Hannibal and hero of the Second Carthaginian War. For Cato see i. 14 n.

unnoticed and unwept: a mistranslation. The expression actually means 'out of sight, unheard of', and is a quotation from Homer's *Odyssey* (i. 242).

what then is that . . . this one thing: cf. ii. 17; v. 33.

35 For the thought and expression cf. vii. 21; viii. 21.

36 *unscientific*: better 'amateurish, unphilosophic': cf. iv. 3, 50; v. 8 (where 'quite simple folk' should be 'amateurs' or 'non-philosophers').

41 *as Epictetus used to say*: the saying (fr. 26 Schenkl) is not in Epictetus' extant works. Marcus had clearly read the books of Epictetus which we have lost.

43 For the river image, compare ii. 17; v. 23; vi. 15. It may derive from the Pre-Socratic philosopher Heraclitus (e.g. fr. B49A), who was an important influence upon the Stoics.

46 The quotations from Heraclitus are frs. B 76, 71–4 Diels–Kranz. For the thought, cf. Marcus himself in iv. 29.

48 *entire cities . . .*: again a commonplace of consolation-literature and other moralistic works; cf. Servius Sulpicius to Cicero, in Cicero's *Letters to his Friends*, IV. v. 4; Lucretius, vi. 585–90; Seneca, *Letters*, xci. 9 ff.

a spot of albumen: peculiarly unclear even for Farquharson. Marcus obviously means sperm: cf. vi. 13.

50 *Caedicianus . . .*: none of those named here are certainly indentifiable.

Book V

1 *When you dislike being called*: cf. ii. 1; there are also a number of references in the historian Dio Cassius to

Marcus' insomnia. Self-indulgent slumber is castigated in Stoic moralistic terms by the satirist Persius (*Satires*, iii. 1 ff.; v. 132 ff.).

the plants, the birds, the ants . . .: ancient moralists often point to the natural world and the animal kingdom to draw lessons for mankind: cf. ix. 9; Cicero, *On the Nature of the Gods*, i. 79; iii. 21; Proverbs 6: 6 'go to the ant, thou sluggard; consider her ways, and be wise'.

6 *doesn't know that he has done it*: the text here is Farquharson's own emendation. Also possible is 'doesn't make a song and dance about it'.

7 *A prayer . . .*: how one should pray was a subject of philosophic discussion in antiquity: cf. Plato, *Alcibiades II*; Horace, *Odes*, I. xxxi; Persius, *Satire ii*, and especially Juvenal, *Satire x* (freely imitated by Dr Johnson as *The Vanity of Human Wishes*).

8 *Aesculapius*: the Greek god of healing, also called Asclepius. He had a famous cult centre at Epidaurus. Patients were often instructed through their dreams while residing there: the cures prescribed might be drastic and bizarre, as Marcus remarks later in the chapter. One famous patient whose record of his own dream-cures is preserved was Aelius Aristides, a distinguished sophist of Marcus' own time: see E. R. Dodds, *Pagan and Christian in an Age of Anxiety*, 39–45.

10 *a few and those not insignificant thinkers*: notably the Sceptics, who asserted the impossibility of knowledge. See A. A. Long, *Hellenistic Philosophy*, ch. 3.

bestial: literally 'catamite'.

in such a fog and filth . . .: here we see Marcus at his most pessimistic, and as often death is regarded as a release or purification from the imperfections and confusion of this life. This attitude, however, is scarcely orthodox Stoicism.

12 *the comic poet*: Menander, *The Ghost*, 42 Sandbach: 'You've

so many good things that you've no room to ease yourself'. Already in Menander it is referred to as a popular expression.

13 *finite periods*: Marcus refers to the cyclical theory according to which, at the end of a long period sometimes referred to as a Great Year, the Universe will be resolved into its elements and then renewed. The idea is also referred to in vi. 32, x. 7, and xi. 1. See further Cicero, *On the Nature of the Gods*, ii. 118; A. A. Long and D. N. Sedley, *The Hellenistic Philosophers*, i. 274–9.

16 *dyed by its imaginations*: cf. vi. 30, and for a different image vii. 3.

it is also possible to live well in a palace: for signs of discontent with the life of the court, cf. vi. 12; viii. 9. But contrast xi. 7.

it has been proved long ago: not by Marcus; phrases such as this one no doubt refer to earlier Stoic textbooks.

18 *exhibits greatness of soul*: the translation is misleading here: the verb is much more pejorative ('is showing off'); similarly in the next sentence 'vanity' would be better than 'complaisance'. There is no need to suppose anything lost at the end.

20 Cf. iv. 1.

22 *the city*: i.e. the world city of which all men are citizens, rather than Rome. Still, the passage obviously has political implications of a general kind. Cf. ii. 16 n.; vi. 54.

23 For the imagery see ii. 17; iv. 43 n.

26 On 'sympathy' see iv. 27 n.

27 *the deity, the portion of himself* . . .: cf. ii. i n.; xii. 26 and 30.

28 *Are you angry* . . .: note here, as elsewhere, the hint of irritation with his associates. Cf. ii. 1.

reasonable disposition: as men are rational beings, they should be able to persuade one another into better courses (viii. 59), and Marcus asserts his own willingness to be persuaded by others: iv. 12; vi. 21; viii. 16. For the value placed on plain speaking, see i. 6, 14. But vi. 50 and 55 show more impatience.

29 *The chimney smokes* . . .: the image comes from Epictetus (I. xxv. 28, cf. IV. x. 27) and means that suicide offers a way out if it becomes impossible to lead a satisfactory moral life. Cf. iii. 1 n.

30 For the thought, cf. v. 16.

31 This review of duties performed or neglected is one of the passages which most clearly shows the similarity between Marcus' work and the perusal of the day's actions recommended by Pythagoras and practised by Horace (*Satires*, I. iv. 133–9), Seneca (*On Anger*, iii. 36) and others: see Rutherford, *The* Meditations *of Marcus Aurelius: A Study*, ch. 1.

not to have wrought . . .: the quotation is an unmetrical adaptation of Homer, *Odyssey*, iv. 690.

your service accomplished: the conception of life as a period of (military) service from which God releases us at the time of death goes back to Plato (*Apology*, 28d, *Phaedo*, 61e) and was generally popular. It is adopted by Christianity: e.g. Ephesians 6: 12, 1 Peter 2: 11.

33 For the reflection on life's transience, cf. iv. 33; viii. 25.

fled to Olympus . . .: the quotation is from Hesiod, *Works and Days*, 197 (in which Self-Respect and Reproach abandon the sinful world).

if the sensible is ever-changing . . . for the instability of life, cf. ii. 17.

extinction or a change of state: for the alternatives, see iii. 3; iv. 21; viii. 25; xi. 3; Socrates in Plato, *Apology*, 40c–41c.

to bear them and to forbear: this adapts a motto of Epictetus (fr. 10 Schenkl; cf. IV. viii. 20).

36 *like the old man* . . .: perhaps a reference to an episode in comedy or mime.

lamenting in the pulpit: not a very happy modernism. The

text is uncertain here; if Farquharson is right, it might be rendered 'when as it is, you are shouting aloud on the orator's platform' (Latin *rostra*)—that is, making a scene about something unimportant.

sufferers: an overtranslation. Perhaps just 'to these people'. But the sense here is generally unclear.

Book VI

2 *one of the acts of life*: cf. Seneca, *Letters*, lxxvii. 19.

4 The uncertainty between alternative views is common: cf. next note.

10 The alternatives posed are again Epicurean atomism and Stoic providence: cf. iv. 3 n.

   return to earth: apparently an unknown quotation.

12 *palace*: for Marcus' attitude to the court, see i. 16–17; v. 16 n.

   and you tolerable in it: note the twist at the end of the chapter, as Marcus shifts from criticism of life in a palace to criticism of himself.

13 *in matters of sex intercourse*: again a rather obscure and prudish rendering by Farquharson; but the technical, quasi-scientific vocabulary is quite appropriate to Marcus' own ruthless reductionism here. For such 'realism', often passing into disgust, cf. ii. 2; viii. 24, 37; ix. 36. In vii. 47 contemplation of the stars is said to purify 'the filth of life on the ground'. In xi. 6 Marcus approves the 'instructive freedom of speech' of Old Comedy and the Cynics, and the procedure he follows is akin to the plain-speaking, even obscene diatribes of the Cynics and of satire.

   Crates . . . Xenocrates: this anecdote is now lost.

14 *stress*: here a technical term from Stoic physics, which might be rendered 'physical coherence' (Haines). See Long and Sedley, *The Hellenistic Philosophers*, i. 280 ff., who normally render it 'tenor'.

15 For the river, cf. ii. 17; iv. 43 n.; vii. 19

16 *To transpire like plants . . .*: for the thought, cf. iii. 16.

　What, then, should be valued?: cf. ii. 17: 'what, then, can be his escort through life? One thing and one only, philosophy . . .'

23 *in all things call upon the gods for help*: cf. i. 17, especially the ending.

24 The equality of death is a commonplace of epitaphs and the like: cf. Lucretius iii. 1065, Horace, *Odes*, I. iv 13 f., etc. But the reference to Alexander the Great has additional force for another emperor.

　life-giving principles . . . atoms: again the Stoic *v.* the Epicurean view.

26 Clear evidence that Marcus is writing for himself: 'you' is self-address here and elsewhere, not a reference to a specific addressee or to the general reading public. Cf. vi. 44.

30 *not to be transformed into a Caesar*: a fascinating allusion to the potential corruption brought about by absolute power. The idea is also prominent in Tacitus: see esp. *Annals*, vi. 48, where it is applied to Tiberius.

　a pupil of Antoninus . . .: on the relation between this sketch and the fuller account of his predecessor in book i, see Introduction, p. xvi.

32 *body and spirit*: contrast the categories in iii. 16.

　understanding: in this context = 'spirit'.

35 *his own principle*: that is, reason.

36 *even the lion's jaws . . .*: cf. and contrast iii. 2.

　secondary consequences . . . by-products: for the ideas implied here, see viii. 50 n.

37 Cf. ii. 14; iv. 32, etc.

38 *stress-movement . . .*: cf. vi. 14 n.

42 *Heraclitus*: fr. B75 Diels–Kranz.

　Chrysippus: SVF (*Stoicorum Veterum Fragmenta*), ii. 1181 (quoted by Plutarch, *Moral Writings*, 1065D): ' "for just as comedies," he says, "contain funny lines which, while vulgar in themselves, add a certain charm to the piece as a whole, so vice all by itself you could censure, but for the universe as a whole it is not useless" ' (tr. H. Cherniss, Loeb edition). See Long and Sedley, *The Hellenistic Philosophers*, i. 383–6.

43 *The Fruit-bearing goddess*: Ceres, also called Demeter, goddess of harvest and fertility.

44 Whether the gods took account of the needs of individuals or were concerned only for the good of the cosmos as a whole was a much-debated question: see e.g. Cicero, *On the Nature of the Gods*, ii. 164; iii. 86; Long and Sedley, *The Hellenistic Philosophers*, i. 327 ff.

or else let us cease to sacrifice . . .: prayer and sacrifice would be pointless if there were no possibility of the gods giving way to individual pleas. For the argument, compare Cicero, *On the Nature of the Gods*, i. 116, 122; Virgil, *Aeneid*, iv. 208 ff.

present and living in our midst: for these beliefs see R. Lane Fox, *Pagans and Christians*, ch. 4.

my city . . . the Universe: see notes on ii. 16 and iv. 29; x. 15.

45 *advantage must be taken in its more usual acceptance*: this is meaningless in English, and would be improved by amendment to 'in its more conventional sense'. Marcus is contrasting the popular view (according to which wealth, health, etc., are advantageous) and the Stoic view (which holds that because they do not affect one's moral state, they are 'indifferent', neither good nor evil).

46 *the amphitheatre*: from the Fronto correspondence (no. 14 in the Appendix) we learn that Marcus sometimes read his mail at the games and gave rise to criticism by his indifference to the popular amusements. It is striking here that he does not criticize the games on moral grounds, but only because they bore him: contrast Seneca, *Letters* vii, or Augustine, *Confessions*, vi. 13. For other references to the Games see x. 8.

how long will it last?: for this *taedium vitae*, cf. ix. 14; ix. 28; Seneca, *Letters*, xxiv. 26.

47 For the chapter's thought and structure, cf. iii. 3; iv. 48 n.
    Philistion, Phoebus, and Origanio are unknown,
    presumably recently dead. Eudoxus was a distinguished
    Hellenistic mathematician and astronomer (fourth century
    BC). Hipparchus was an astronomer of the second century
    BC. Archimedes of course remains one of the most famous
    mathematicians of the ancient world (d. 212 BC). Menippus
    is a more literary figure, a Cynic who wrote humorous skits
    with a philosophic message. His works are lost, but we can
    see something of what they were like through Lucian's
    imitations and adaptations: just how much Lucian took
    from him is hotly disputed.

48 As discussed in the introduction, this chapter seems to set
    the programme for book i. It is notable that Marcus takes
    a warmer view of his associates here than in many other
    passages: contrast esp. v. 10.

50 *with a reservation*: Marcus means that although he hoped to
    achieve the aim he had in mind, he was always aware that
    he might not be successful. For the Stoics, what mattered
    was not the success of an action, but the moral attitude with
    which it was undertaken.

53 Cf. vii. 4 and 30.

55 *spoke evil of the master of the ship* . . .: there is an implicit
    analogy with those who speak ill of Marcus himself, the cap-
    tain of the ship of state, the physician of the body politic.

Book VII

2 *Your principles are living principles. How else* . . .: the text
   is doubtful here. The opening of the chapter may be all one
   sentence: 'how can your principles ever perish unless the
   images . . .'

3 For the colourful imagery used here to describe life, cf. iv.
   32; vii. 48; Seneca, *On the resolution of the sage*, xii. 2; *On
   calm of mind*, xii. 3; Epictetus, IV. vii. 19–24.

5 *withdraw*: by abdication or suicide?

7 *like a soldier in a storming-party*: on the metaphor of life as military service, see v. 31 n.

12 Cf. the ending of iii. 5; also vii. 7 above.

13 The point of the chapter depends on the similarity of two Greek words: *melos* (limb) and *meros* (part, portion). Cf. vii. 74.

19 *Chrysippus*: *c.*280–207 BC; one of the most important of the early heads of the Stoic school.

22 *to love even those who stumble*: this does not quite go as far as the fellow-feeling recommended in the Gospels (e.g. Matthew 5:44 'but I say unto you, love your enemies, bless them that curse you').

because of ignorance: cf. ii. 1 n.

24 *the consciousness of doing wrong*: i.e. conscience. For ancient conceptions of conscience see esp. H. Chadwick, in *Reallexicon für Antike und Christentum*, 10 (Stuttgart, 1978), 1025 ff., R. Parker, *Miasma* (Oxford, 1983), 252 ff.

25 *ever fresh and young*: for this theme of regeneration cf. vi. 15; also viii. 50; xii. 23.

26 *you will pity him*: cf. vi. 27; vii. 22; 65; ix. 3. Marcus is kinder than the dogma of the Old Stoa would allow; as Cicero's witty parody in the speech *In Defence of Murena* (61–6) shows, the ideal Stoic should be unswayed by these softer emotions.

28 *withdraw into yourself*: iv. 3 n.

29 Note the accumulation of brief imperatives and aphorisms, some of which may be found elsewhere in the work (ix. 20, 38, etc.).

31 *Democritus*: not actually named in the Greek, which vaguely says 'that man says that . . .'. The reference could be to frs. B9, 117, 125. The text and interpretation of this chapter are doubtful.

33 *what we cannot bear . . . borne*: this paraphrases Epicurus fr. 447 Usener.

35 This and several of the next series of chapters consist of quotations. This one is from Plato, *Republic*, 486a.

36 Antisthenes, fr. 20b Caizzi; also quoted by Epictetus, IV. vi. 20. See A. S. Riginos, *Platonica* (Leiden, 1976), 99.

37 For 'absurd' read 'shameful'.

38 Euripides, *Bellerophon*, fr. 287. 1 ff. Nauck, also quoted in xi. 6.

39 A quotation from an unknown source.

40 Euripides, *Hypsipyle*, fr. 757. 6 ff., a classic anthology piece. Cf. Cicero, *Tusculan Disputations*, iii. 59; Epictetus, II. vi. 14.

41 Euripides, *Antiope*, fr. 208. 1 f. Again also quoted in xi. 6.

42 Euripides, fr. 918. 3 ff.

43 Source unknown.

44-6 Preceded in one of the manuscripts by the Greek for 'Platonic passages'.

44 Plato, *Apology*, 28b.

45 Ibid., 28d. Note the motif of *militia vitae* (life as military service), used by Marcus elsewhere (v. 31 n.).

46 Plato, *Gorgias*, 512d-e.

47 Cf. xi. 27 for the same idea of purity in the heavens contrasted with foulness on earth.

48 Cf. vii. 3 n. But here the idea of *order* is present, despite mixture and confusion.

50 Euripides, *Chrysippus*, fr. 839. 9-11.

51 Euripides, *Suppliants*, 1110-1, and an unknown fragment.

55 *inferior . . . superior*: cf. v. 16, 30; xi. 10. This was regular Stoic doctrine.

58 *material*: that is, raw material on which to exercise his moral judgement. Cf. vii. 68; viii. 35.

59 Cf. viii. 51.

60 Physiognomy and style of walking often have moral implications in ancient thinking. See further vii. 27, 34, and esp. xi. 15; E. Evans, *Harvard Studies in Classical Philology*, 46 (1935), 43-84.

63 *he says*: 'he' is Plato, but as paraphrased by Epictetus, I. xxviii. 4. *Republic*, 412e–3a and *Sophist*, 228c are close, but the doctrine is one which permeates Plato's work.

64 Epicurus, fr. 447, already paraphrased in vii. 33.

66 *Telauges*: a very shadowy figure, who appeared in a lost dialogue by Aeschines, one of Socrates' less well-known disciples. Without the dialogue, it is doubtful whether we can ever make sense of this allusion.

frosty night: see the anecdote told in Plato, *Symposium*, 220.

Leo of Salamis: see Plato, *Apology*, 32c.

carried his head high in the streets: a quotation from Aristophanes, *Clouds*, 362, a passage making fun of Socrates' strutting gait. It is also jocularly quoted by a speaker in Plato, *Symposium*, 221b.

69 Cf.ii. 5; vii. 56, etc.

70 *they care for them in all kinds of ways*: cf.ix. 40; ix. 27 and n. ('dreams . . . prophecy').

73 For the idea, cf. v. 6.

75 *either . . . or*: the second alternative is regarded as an impossibility.

Book VIII

1 *your calling, too . . .*: but contrast viii. 9.

where then is it to be found?: for the movement of the argument cf. ii. 17, etc.

3 Kings and tyrants are here contrasted with philosophers. For the dismissal of the tyrants as blind or deluded compare esp. iii. 3; ix. 29.

4 *they*: the ignorant, those who do not follow the path of philosophy.

8 The chapter contrasts intellectual pursuits (which require time to treat seriously) and moral action (which is possible at all times).

12 *sleep*: cf. ii. 1 and v. 1, with n.

13 *natural science* . . .: the traditional tripartite division of philosophy.

14 Cf.v. 17.

15 For the fig image, cf. iv. 6; for the physician and captain, vi. 55.

16 For the willingness to be shown to be wrong, cf. iv. 12; v. 28 n.

19 *To please yourself*: (or 'for pleasure'). This was the view of the Epicureans.

21 *A mere point*: cf. iii. 10 n.; iv. 3, 14; vi. 36.

24 Cf. ix. 36. The loathing for the physical world is strikingly contrary to mainstream Stoicism: contrast e.g. the Stoic speaker in Cicero, *On the Nature of the Gods*, ii. 75 '(the second part of the argument is) the part which proves that all things are under the control of a sentient nature, and that nature's works are all of the utmost beauty'. See Dodds, *Pagan and Christian in an Age of Anxiety*, 29ff. (criticized by Lane Fox, *Pagans and Christians*, 360 ff.).

25 Lucilla: mother of Marcus? Verus is either her husband, Marcus' natural father, or Marcus' co-emperor who died in AD 169. Maximus: see i. 15. Secunda was presumably his wife. Celer: rhetorical tutor of Marcus and Verus, not mentioned in book i but included in the longer lists of teachers in the *Augustan History*. Hadrianus: perhaps the sophist of that name (Philostratus, *Lives of the Sophists*, ii. 10). Epitynchanos and Diotimus are unknown. Demetrius: a Platonist of the day (Lucian, *On Slander*, 16). Charax: unknown, unless the same man as a philosopher of Pergamum: see A. B. Bosworth, *From Arrian to Alexander* (Oxford, 1988), 24–5. Eudaemon: unknown.

28 *quiet and calm*: the Greek conveys more of a seagoing metaphor. Cf. xii. 22.

30 Stylistic simplicity is closely related to sincerity, in Stoic theory and in ethical treatments of literature more generally

Marcus' name Verus ('true') was expanded by Hadrian to Verissimus ('truest of men'), and many references in the *Meditations* indicate the value he placed on openness and sincerity: see esp. xi. 15.

31 *Areios*: distinguished philosopher resident in Rome at the court of Augustus; he composed work of Stoic tenor, known and read by Seneca and others.

Maecenas: one of Augustus' closest friends and advisers in the earlier stages of his reign; most famous as the patron and friend of Virgil, Horace, and Propertius. See further J. Griffin, in *Caesar Augustus: Seven Aspects*, ed. F. Millar and E. Segal (Oxford, 1984), 189–218.

34 *If you have ever seen a dismembered hand or foot . . .*: does this reflect personal experience? For the thought, cf. xi. 8.

37 *Panthea*: a famous courtesan, mistress of Marcus' co-emperor Verus. See C. P. Jones, *Culture and Society in Lucian* (Cambridge Mass., 1986), ch. 7.

Pergamos: probably a freedman or favourite of Verus.

Chabrias and Diotimus: favourites of Hadrian? Otherwise unknown (cf. 25).

38 *says he*: the text is uncertain, but if this is right, the author is unknown.

41 *a sphere rounded and at rest*: the phrase comes from the Pre-Socratic poet and thinker Empedocles (B 27. 4 = 28. 2). For the sphere as the perfect form see xi. 12; xii. 3. Horace, *Satires*, II. vii. 86 and Seneca, *Apocolocyntosis*, viii. 1 make fun of the idea.

47 *Depart then from life*: by suicide, cf. iii. 1 n.

48 *invincible*: cf. 41.

citadel: for the image, cf. Cicero, *Tusculan Disputations*, ii. 58; Epictetus, IV. i. 86; IV. v. 25 ff.

50 *shavings and clippings*: according to an argument used by Chrysippus, the ugly and undesirable things in the world are the unfortunate left overs from God's workshop, like the

sawdust in a carpenter's shop. See *SVF*, ii. 1178; Long and Sedley, *The Hellenistic Philosophers*, i. 330.

51 *They kill you . . .*: implausibly taken by some to refer to the persecution of the Christians. For a detailed refutation of this view, see the article by P. A. Brunt cited on xi. 3.

sweet and crystal spring . . . The image is an expanded version of vii. 69. Cf. Plutarch, *On Calm of Mind*, 467a; Mark 7: 15; John 4: 13–6.

52 Cf. iv. 29.

57 *extension . . . extended*: the point is the resemblance between the Greek words for 'rays' (*aktines*) and 'extend' (*ekteinein*); but the etymology is in fact a false one.

Book IX

2 *the plague*: possibly an allusion to the disastrous plague that Verus and his armies brought back from the East in the late 160s.

a plague to animals: it should be made clear that 'animals' here includes mankind.

3 *the unborn child . . . your wife's womb*: it is uncertain whether this is a personal reference to Marcus' own wife and child. On his offspring see A. R. Birley, *Marcus Aurelius* (revised edn., 1987), Appendix 2, esp. 247–8.

the kind of characters: cf. v. 10.

like-minded: cf. and contrast the thought of xi. 8.

9 *there were found from the first . . .*: the account of early human and animal history bears some resemblance to more ambitious historical reconstructions such as the fifth book of Lucretius. See in general W. K. C. Guthrie, *In the Beginning* (Ithaca NY, 1957); E. R. Dodds, *The Ancient Concept of Progress and other essays* (Oxford, 1973), ch. 1.

nature is too strong for them: cf. Cleanthes, *SVF*, i. 527, who declares that even those who seek to disobey the divine will find themselves obeying it despite themselves; similarly

Seneca, *Letters*, cvii. 11, 'ducunt volentem fata, nolentem trahunt' ('destiny guides the willing on their path, drags the unwilling').

11 *the gods, too, are kind . . .*: cf. 27.

15 The meaning is that it is up to the individual to make his own assessment of circumstances, which are themselves indifferent. Cf. e. g. viii. 47.

20 Cf. vii. 29; ix. 38.

21 Cf. 3. For the argument compare also Seneca, *Consolation to Marcia*, xxi. 6.

22 *whether it is ignorance or design*: sc. that makes him act wrongly in the way he does.

24 *spirits carrying dead bodies*: an allusion to the saying of Epictetus quoted in iv. 41.

story of the visit . . .: Marcus refers to Odysseus' encounter with the bloodless ghosts of his mother and friends in book xi of Homer's *Odyssey*. The point of the chapter is that human life around Marcus seems as trivial and insubstantial as the world of the dead.

27 *dreams . . . prophecy*: cf. Marcus in a letter to Fronto, Appendix, no. 4; also the reference to help he himself has had through dreams (*Meditations*, i. 17, near the end). In general on prophetic dreams and visions, see R. Lane Fox, *Pagans and Christians*, 149–166. Ancient books on how to interpret dreams are still extant, especially that of Artemidorus of Dalda (Lane Fox, 155–8); note also the case of Aelius Aristides (v. 8 n. above).

29 *Plato's Utopia*: the ideal state fantastically constructed in the *Republic*. Plato's vision was a byword for its impracticality: Cicero complains of the Stoic Cato that 'he acts as if he's living in Plato's ideal state instead of this cess-pit of Romulus's' (*Letters to Atticus*, II. i. 8).

how cheap . . . drivel: in the manuscript this sentence follows 'all in its stream', the first sentence of the chapter. Farquharson transposed it to the position it occupies here; it is debatable whether this is an improvement.

these mere men with their policies: it is unclear who is meant: perhaps advisers and flatterers who pretended philosophic allegiances in the hope of pleasing Marcus?

Philip, and Demetrius of Phalerum: Philip was king of Macedon, father of Alexander the Great, assassinated in 336 BC. Demetrius (born *c.* 350 BC) was a pro-Macedonian overlord of Athens, eventually expelled and reviled after his fall from power.

actors on the world's stage: rather, 'played their grandiose roles'. Cf.iii. 8; v. 28.

30 Cf. iv. 48; viii. 25.

32 *embracing in your thought the whole Universe*: for the idea of the philosophic imagination and its vast grasp, cf. Lucretius, i. 72–9; Horace, *Odes*, I, xxviii. 1 ff.

34 *in nakedness*: so too God can look at human souls 'stripped of their material vessels and coverings and dross' (xii. 2); cf. Plato, *Gorgias*, 523.

35 *So no power . . .*: cf. xii. 5: if it were better that things should be different, the gods would surely have made them so.

36 Cf. viii. 24 n.; vi. 13.

39 *atoms*: the Epicurean view again. Cf. iv. 27 n.; vi. 10; vii. 32; xii. 14.

40 *the gods put these things in my power*: doctrinally interesting: can they, then, or will they, grant divine aid to men ('grace')?

besides, who told you that the gods . . .: this idea is unorthodox for Stoics. Cf. Matthew 5: 28. In general, see Long and Sedley, *The Hellenistic Philosophers*, i. 386 ff. on Stoic discussion of the nature of moral responsibility.

41 Epicurus, fr. 191, cf. Diogenes Laertius, *Lives of the Philosophers*, x. 22. From a letter written in his final illness. Notice the harmony between Stoics and Epicureans in their concern for resolute confrontation of death.

in illness: it is worth remembering that Marcus was often ill. Cf. i. 15 (opening); Dio Cassius LXXII. xxiv. 4, xxxvi. 2. In

i. 17 Marcus thanks the gods for allowing his body to hold out so long in such a life.

42 The whole chapter is a good example of Marcus' capacity for sustained argument, and brings together a number of key ideas in the *Meditations*.

do not then ask for the impossible: cf. v. 17.

bestowed a favour: cf. v. 6.

eye . . . feet . . .: for the analogy between bodily parts and man as a part of the social order, cf.ii. 1; also see ii. 16 and iv. 27 n.

BOOK X

6 *atoms*: Epicurean doctrine, cf.iv. 27 n.

nothing which benefits the Whole . . .: cf.vi. 54.

7 *whether did . . . or*: impossible in English. The simplest improvement is to delete 'whether'.

periodically: again a reference to the idea of the cosmic cycle or 'great year': v. 13 n.

8 *changed man . . . changed life*: cf.vii. 2.

arena: for Marcus' disgust at the Games see vi. 46 and n.

depart altogether from life: cf.iii. 1 n.

but simply: cf. xi. 3 and n.

to be made into their likeness: the idea of imitating and becoming like the gods comes from Plato (*Theaetetus*, 176b).

10 *Sarmatian prisoners*: presumably a reference to Marcus' own campaigns against this Germanic tribe. See Dio Cassius, LXXI. xvii; *Augustan History, Life of Marcus*, xxiv-v. Marcus assumed the title *Sarmaticus* in AD 175.

15 *as in a city*: again the Stoic idea of a cosmopolis. Cf.ii. 16 (with n.); iii. 11; xii. 36, etc.

21 *Earth loves . . .*: Euripides, fr. 898 Nauck.

22 *your service*: see v. 31 n.

23 *what Plato says*: the allusion is to Plato, *Theaetetus*, 174d, part of a famous passage contrasting the philosopher with the man of affairs or rhetorician. The relevance of the quotation is not clear. In Plato, the phrase quoted describes the philosopher's opinion of a hypothetical much-praised ruler: 'he fancies he is hearing some keeper of swine or sheep or cows being congratulated on the quantity of milk he has squeezed out of his flock . . . and that a herdsman of this sort, penned up in his castle, is doomed by sheer press of work to be as rude and uncultivated as the shepherd in his mountain fold.' There are certainly analogies here to Marcus' situation and what he sometimes feels about it.

26 A very unusual subject for Marcus, and a remarkable mixture of warm, human terms and scientific/medical terminology.

27 *whole dramas and scenes*: for life as a play, see xii. 36 n. Also ix. 29 (Alexander, etc., as tragic actors).

   Philip: ix. 29 n.

   Croesus: proverbially wealthy king of Lydia, overthrown by Cyrus the Great of Persia in 547–46 BC. His story is narrated in the first book of Herodotus' *Histories*.

28 *mere obedience is necessary for all*: because destiny compels even the reluctant to obey her demands; see ix. 9 n.

31 *Satyrion . . . Severus*: a cluster of unknowns with a few famous names (Xenophon the Greek historian, Crito the friend of Socrates, Euphrates the sophist—for the last, see Pliny, *Letters*, i. 10). But the main point is clear from the second sentence; for the thought, cf. iv. 32–3, 48, 50; viii. 25, 31.

   smoke and nothingness: cf. xii. 33.

   school of exercise: this alludes to a theory prominent in Seneca, that hardships and misfortune are put in the world for men to practise virtue by overcoming them: see e.g. Seneca, *On the Resolution of the Sage* and Epictetus. I. xxiv.

   bright fire: cf. iv. 1.

32 *not to go on living*: see iii. 1 n.

33 *a roller on a slope*: a stock illustration of the force of necessity, used by the Stoic Chrysippus, *SVF*, ii. 1000: 'just as if you push a stone cylinder on steeply sloping ground, you have produced the cause and beginning of a forward motion, but soon it rolls forward not because you are still making it do so, but because such are its form and smooth-rolling shape—so too the order, rationale, and necessity of fate sets in motion the actual types of causes and their beginnings, but the deliberate impulses of our minds and our actual actions are controlled by our individual will and intellect' (Long and Sedley, *The Hellenistic Philosophers*, i. 388).

34 For Marcus on the didactic value of poetry, see xi. 6 and n.

leaves, the wind . . . men: an abbreviated version of Homer, *Iliad*, vi. 146–9, a famous passage, much quoted and imitated: cf. Plutarch, *Moral Works*, 104E, 560C; Virgil, *Aeneid*, vi. 309 ff.; Milton, *Paradise Lost*, i.302 f.

another will be lamenting: cf.iv. 43.

36 *earnest and wise . . . earnest*: Farquharson's translation somewhat obscures the fact that Marcus is speaking of the Stoic sage or *sapiens*, in contrast with a lesser man like himself.

38 *that what is hidden within*: that is, the governing self, as opposed to the body: cf. iii. 3; xii. 1, etc.

BOOK XI

1 *in every scene of life . . .*: xii. 36 n.

surveys its shape: cf.ix. 32.

periodic rebirth: the theory of a cyclical universe: see v. 13 n.

2 For the method prescribed, see vi. 13 and n.

3 *from a specific decision*: cf. iii. 1 n., and the parallels cited there. Marcus would not approve of a man taking his life out of despair or as a gesture (cf. x. 8).

not out of sheer opposition like the Christians: the point is that, as a famous policy letter from the emperor Trajan to Pliny makes clear, Christians could easily escape martyrdom for their beliefs if they were prepared to recant, and to prove their change of heart by sacrificing to the emperor. Their regular refusal to do so seemed absurd obstinacy to the non-Christian. See further R. Lane Fox, *Pagans and Christians*, 419 ff.

This is the only explicit reference to the Christians in the *Meditations*; they clearly did not bulk large in the emperor's horizon, and it has been argued that at this date the sect may not have gained any special prominence in the West. See esp. P. A. Brunt, 'Marcus Aurelius and the Christians', in *Studies in Latin Literature and Roman History*, ed. C. Deroux, i (Brussels, 1979), 483 ff. His further argument, that in this passage 'like the Christians' should be deleted as a later addition, is less persuasive.

6 One of the most interesting of Marcus' reflections for the literary critic. Notice the firmly didactic, moral view of poetry's function and effect, in each genre. This was part of the Stoics' inheritance from Plato's stern strictures on poetry.

the world's greater stage: see xii. 36 n.

The quotations are first ('*Alas* . . .') Sophocles, *Oedipus the King*, 1391, then a selection of those quoted in vii. 38–41; see notes there.

Old Comedy: as practised by Aristophanes. New Comedy is represented for us by Menander; of other Greek comic authors, and of Middle Comedy as a whole, we have only fragmentary remains. See R. L. Hunter, *The New Comedy of Ancient Greece and Rome* (Cambridge, 1984).

Diogenes: the famous Cynic philosopher, renowned for his satirical tongue. See Diogenes Laertius, *Lives of the Philosophers*, vi. 20–81.

7 On Marcus' attitude to the court, see v. 16 n. The thought here is a sharp conflict with the view of Agrippina, Nero's mother, in Suetonius, *Nero*, 52: 'his mother turned him from

philosophy, warning him that it was a hindrance to a future ruler'; contrast also Lucan, viii.492–3: 'exeat aula / qui volt esse pius; virtus et summa potestas / non coeunt' ('let the man who wishes to be good depart from court; virtue and supreme power do not mix').

8 Cf. esp. viii. 34. But the thought in this passage is more pessimistic: reunion after repeated schism cannot be a *true* unity.

10 *No Nature* . . .: an unknown quotation expressing a doctrine found in Aristotle (*Physics*, 194a 21); cf. also Cicero, *On the Nature of the Gods*, ii. 81.

12 *sphere*: see viii. 41 n.

13 *Phocion*: a fourth-century BC Athenian statesman, who enjoyed remarkable military and political success but was eventually condemned to death in 318 BC. His colourful career is narrated in a biography by Plutarch. The story alluded to here comes in Plutarch, *Phocion*, 36 and in other sources: when about to be executed, Phocion was asked if he had any message to send to his son, and replied, 'Yes, tell him not to bear a grudge against the Athenians over my death.'

15 For the interest in facial expression as a sign of character, see vii. 37 n.

a razor: rather, a concealed knife. Haines's rendering 'a stiletto' is preferable, as the word is Thracian and should sound foreign and dangerous.

18 The longest chapter in the *Meditations* outside book i. It is almost a disjointed sermon on anger, a frequent topic in ancient moral discussion, and one which is explored more systematically in treatises by Seneca and Plutarch. Marcus' treatment is analysed in detail and compared with theirs by P. A. Brunt, *Journal of Roman Studies*, 64 (1974), 10–12. Notice the frequency with which we meet themes which appear separately elsewhere in the *Meditations*.

if it be not sneering [better, *fawning*] *or hypocritical*: for the concern for sincerity, cf. xi. 15.

not as if you were lecturing him . . .: cf.x. 36 (the schoolmaster image).

it is aiming at the impossible: cf.iv. 6; v. 17, etc.

19 *your more divine part* . . .: cf.ii. 13; iii.3 (end), etc.

from the other world: overtranslated (more accurately 'from over there'), but on the right lines. It is remarkable that Marcus allows himself to stray so near to a non-Stoic dualism. Cf.ii. 17.

22 *the mountain mouse and the town mouse*: Aesop 297 Halm; Horace, *Satires*, II. vi (see N. Rudd, *The Satires of Horace* (Cambridge, 1966), ch. 9). Why the fable is so allusively mentioned here is not plain; perhaps another dismissive description of human life? (Cf. vii. 3, 'scurrying of startled mice'.)

23 From Epictetus, II, i. 15; cf. III. xxii. 105ff.; Plato, *Crito*, 46e, *Phaedo*, 77e are close but not exactly the same. In Greek the 'Bogies' are Lamiae, monstrous female vampire creatures of ancient folk-tale (e.g. Aristophanes, *Wasps*, 1177).

24 Presumably an example of courteous and sociable behaviour.

25 *Perdiccas*: this is a slip of memory on Marcus' part; the king in question should be Archelaus of Macedon (see Aristotle, *Rhetoric*, 1398a 24). Archelaus was an adventurer who seized power in Macedon by criminal means (Plato, *Gorgias*, 471), then set himself up as a patron of the arts, inviting many distinguished literary figures to his court. Euripides and Agathon both resided there in the last years of the fifth century.

26 Epicurus, fr. 210 Usener; cf. Seneca, *Letters*, xi. 8; xxv. 4–7; Musonius, fr. 11 Hense.

27 Cf.vii. 47–8.

a star has no veil: i.e. no hypocrisy or falsehood.

28 *Xanthippe*: Socrates' wife, who briefly appears in Plato's *Phaedo*. She had the reputation, perhaps derived from

comedy, of being a shrew: see e.g. Xenophon, *Memories of Socrates*, ii. 2; Diogenes Laertius, *Lives of the Philosophers*, ii. 36–7. Here we have a story which illustrates her bullying and his composure.

30 Unknown author, perhaps a tragedian.

31 Homer, *Odyssey*, ix. 413 (Odysseus triumphing over the Cyclops). The relevance of this line to Marcus is irrecoverable.

32 Hesiod, *Works and Days*, 185, moralized by Marcus or his source ('virtue' is not in the authentic text).

33–5 Epictetus, III. xxiv. 86–93, adapted.

36 Epictetus, III. xxii. 105.

37–8 Epictetus, frs. 27 and 28 Schenkl.

39 The thought has nothing un-Socratic about it, but the source is not to be found in Plato or Xenophon.

   Some of these quotations are close to Marcus' regular themes, but the application of chs. 30–1 to his own situation can only be guessed at.

BOOK XII

3 *body, vital spirit, mind*: cf.iii. 16. The language and thought here is reminiscent of Plato's *Phaedo*, according to which the soul will eventually find freedom, but only after it has sloughed off and disentangled itself from the body.

   the sphere of Empedocles: see Empedocles, frs. B27–8 Diels–Kranz; cf. viii. 41 n.

5 A particularly important chapter for Marcus' religious views, both on divine providence and on the question of the after-life; on the latter he would plainly like to believe that the gods have made provision at least for the deserving, but stops short of actually committing himself. See further ii. 3 ('if to a second life, nothing is void of gods, not even in that other world; but if to unconsciousness . . .'); iv. 21; xi. 3. Orthodox Stoicism allowed little scope for individual survival.

8 Another chapter of 'headings', some of which are developed elsewhere. Cf. xii. 26.

14–15 *Either . . . or . . . or . . .*: three conceptions of the Universe. Stoics could express their views in terms of either the first or the second; the third is of course the Epicurean view. But the second allows more scope of divine aid or 'grace': cf. ix. 40 n. and vi. 44.

you have yourself within you . . .: cf. ix. 28.

14–15 are combined in most modern editions, perhaps rightly. There are many such ambiguous cases; Marcus himself may not always have divided his reflections into clearly defined units.

22 *all smoothly strewn . . .*: these last words may be a quotation from an unknown source (cf. i. 17, conclusion).

24 *how great a company of beings . . .*: probably a reference to the heavenly bodies. Alternatively, spirits of the heavens, like the *daimones* popular in philosophic-religious writings at this date (e.g. Plutarch, *On Isis and Osiris*, 360–1).

these *are the objects of your pride*: an unlikely translation. Better: 'and pride as well as these'.

27 *smoke and ashes*: cf.iv. 32; x. 31; xii. 33.

Fabius Catullinus: perhaps the same Fabius as mentioned in the parallel passage at iv. 32. Lusius Lupus is unknown. Stertinius at Baiae: perhaps the rich physician of Naples mentioned by Pliny, *Natural History* xxix. 5. Tiberius in Capri: the emperor Tiberius, weary of ruling, took refuge there in the last years of his reign. Scandal described his life on the island as a horrific saga of depravity. See Tacitus, *Annals*, iv. 57, 67; Suetonius, *Tiberius*, 39–45 and elsewhere. Velius Rufus: a correspondent of Fronto (ii. 86–8 Haines). But the one extant letter to him reveals nothing about his character.

28 *those who ask the question*: The question and the counter-arguments are traditional in theological writing. For 'I have not seen my soul', cf. Cicero, *Tusculan Disputations*, i. 70, Apuleius, *Florida*, 10.

30 For the one-ness of the cosmos, cf. iv. 40.

34 For the thought, cf. Cicero, *Tusculan Disputations*, v. 119–20. Marcus probably thinks especially of Epicurus, whose bravery in his last illness was famous: cf. ix. 41; Seneca, *Letters*, xcii. 25–6; Aulus Gellius, ii. 8.

36 *in this great City*: again, the city is not Rome but the world: cf. ii. 16 n.; iii. 11; iv. 23, 29.

an actor: to be exact, a *comic* actor. So too the emperor Augustus was said to have asked on his death-bed: 'what do you think, friends? Have we played the comedy well?' (Suetonius, *Augustus*, 99, with added details). The image of life as a play is common: cf. Cicero, *On Old Age*, 70; Epictetus, *Handbook*, 17. In Marcus himself cf. iii. 8; vi. 42; vii. 3; ix. 29; x. 27; xi. 1, 6. For a later instance see Gibbon, *The Decline and Fall of the Roman Empire*, ch. 17 (ii. 160 ed. J. B. Bury): 'By a philosophic observer, the system of the Roman government might have been mistaken for a splendid theatre, filled with players of every character and degree, who repeated the language, and imitated the passions, of their original model.'

Correspondence with Fronto

1 The contrast between style for its own sake and ethics is a recurring motif of the correspondence, related to the more polemical conflict between rhetoric and philosophy, to which Fronto often alludes (cf. nos. 12 and 16). Here Marcus regards truthfulness as a finer lesson than literary technique. Veracity was in general a quality he valued highly: it perhaps had special importance to him because his own *cognomen* was 'Verus' ('True'). Cf. the remarks about flatterers in no. 3; and in the *Meditations*, xi. 15; xii. 4.

2 The reference to Fronto as consul provides a firm dating to AD 143, and Marcus' enthusiastic praise seems to be his reaction to his master's speech in honour of Pius, who was then emperor. Several letters from the same year include references to Fronto's painstaking composition of this speech, and no. 15, many years later, shows Fronto proudly remembering it. The speech was actually delivered on 13 August 143 (see i. 112 Haines): for what is known or deducible about it see Champlin, *Fronto and Antonine Rome*, 83–8.

Marcus Porcius Cato: not the Stoic opponent of Julius Caesar (*Meditations*, i. 14 with note), but his great grandfather (234–149 BC), one of the most important politicians of the Republic, famous for his moral severity and his antagonism to Rome's perennial foe Carthage. For an ancient biography see Plutarch, *Cato the Elder* (translated in the Penguin volume *Plutarch: Makers of Rome*); for a modern account, see A. E. Astin, *Cato the Censor* (Oxford, 1978). Like the early epic poets and dramatists, Cato was in vogue with the archaizing movement at Rome under Hadrian and the Antonine monarchs. He is constantly referred to as an authority by Fronto, and Marcus too evidently read him with great enthusiasm; see e.g. i. 152 Haines.

Pheidias: great sculptor of Periclean Athens, famous above all for two gigantic statues now destroyed: that of Athena for the Parthenon, and that of Zeus for the temple at Olympia, his masterpiece.

Apelles: painter of the fourth century BC, who painted Philip, Alexander, and others. A famous painting by Giambattista Tiepolo shows him painting Campaspe, one of Alexander's mistresses.

Demosthenes: (384–322 BC) greatest of Greek orators, and opponent of Philip and Alexander of Macedon.

3 The appeal to Ennius and Naevius, the epic poets of early Rome, and to the early comedian Plautus, as authorities illustrates the vogue of 'archaic' literature in the period of Fronto. It is consistent with this that Marcus seems to have little time for Horace, the great Augustan lyric and satiric poet, who himself had had a low opinion of early Latin verse. The reference to Polemo is to be found in the letter by Fronto to which this is a reply (i. 118 ff. Haines), in which Fronto praises Horace, quoting from his *Satires* a passage describing the 'conversion' of the rake Polemo to virtuous conduct when he accidentally overheard a philosopher lecturing.

   On flatterers, cf. *Meditations*, i. 16 (the chapter praising Pius): '. . . the check in his reign put on organized applause and every form of lip-service,' and many other passages.

4 This birthday greeting is chiefly of interest for the religious invocation, which is couched in a high-flown rhetorical style, no doubt in order to please Fronto. Nevertheless there are points of contact with the *Meditations*: see v. 8 for Aesculapius (god of healing), and for the assistance given by the gods to men through dreams and oracles see i. 17 (near the end), ix. 11, 27, 40, with notes.

5 Anagnia lies in the former territory of the Marsi, somewhat to the East of Rome and near Cicero's native town of Arpinum. The letter excellently shows the antiquarian interests of the period, particularly where early religious rites and symbols are concerned.

all the vine-shoots of the Massic and Gauran vineyards:

'Massic' (Kiessling's emendation) is adopted by Haines and preferable on vinological grounds to 'Marsic'. Both Massic and Gauran wine come from Campania and would be fruity reds, whereas the austere Segnian vine (from Signi, further to the north) was less appealing, but grew better with age. Is there a hinted comparison with the mature wisdom of the older Fronto?

6 One of many passages in which Fronto lectures his pupil on the proper choice of words, and the impropriety of any obscurity or jarring stylistic touch (cf. no. 10). This teaching had its effect: cf. *Meditations*, viii. 30 'Speak both in the senate and to every man of whatever rank with propriety, without affectation. Use words that ring true.' Cf. also iii. 5.

7 Here Marcus is away from Rome, no doubt in one of the imperial villas. Pius had two main family estates, one at Lorium (north of Rome) and one at Lanuvium (cf. *Meditations*, i. 16, 'his costume was brought to Rome from his country house at Lorium; his manner of life at Lanuvium . . .'). Striking here is the zeal with which the scholarly Marcus seems to have participated in the manual labour necessary to bring in the harvest. The biography of Pius in the *Historia Augusta* (vii. 2 and 5) mentions that he liked to spend the vintage-time among friends, like a private citizen, but the sweaty labour described here and in the next letter goes further than that. Normally we would expect the aristocrats simply to be looking on as the peasants laboured. At the same time there are traces of townish sophistication and amused superiority in these letters (esp. no. 8, 'we had fun listening to the country folk jeering at one another'); Horace, *Satires*, I. v is an illuminating parallel.

the ninth hour of the night until the second hour of the day: the Romans generally divided their days into twelve equal parts ('horae') from sunrise to sunset; it followed that these were not, like our hours, of a standard length, but varied according to the season. In modern terms, the 'day' at Rome may vary from just under 9 hours to over 15. When the day and its hours are longest, the hours of the night will be at their shortest. Conversion is often awkward, but here the context shows that Marcus has got up well before dawn to read and work; in the next letter he is still an early riser, but on account of his cold gives himself longer in bed and works for an hour less.

8 Clearly this letter was written the day after no. 7, and continues some of the same themes. For the rapidity of successive letters to the same addressee (more natural in an age which lacked telephones), compare Cicero's correspondence with his close friend Atticus, e.g. the sequence of letters in March of 49 BC, *ad Atticum* book ix (esp. 13-16): in that series, Cicero even opens ix. 16 with the sentence: 'Though I have nothing to say to you I am sending this letter in order not to miss a day'!

The Elder Cato's *On Agriculture* is still extant: for discussion see A. E. Astin (cited under 2 above), ch. 9.

9 The speech in question cannot be certainly identified. The reference to sleep can be connected with a number of other passages in the correspondence which suggest that Marcus already suffered from the insomnia which dogged his later years (*Meditations*, ii. 1; v. 1, etc.; Dio Cassius, lxxi. 34 and 36).

10 The quest for the *mot juste*, and the careful discrimination between words, are leitmotifs of Fronto's teaching, and very prominent in the evidence for this outside the correspondence: see e.g. Aulus Gellius, *Attic Nights*, ii. 26; xiii. 28; xix. 8, 10 (all reproduced in Haines' Loeb edn. of Fronto, ii. 252 ff.). In the Greek world this phenomenon characterizes the literary movement known as 'Atticism', which canonized the classical authors of fifth- and fourth-century Athens to the extent of demanding that the modern speaker's vocabulary should be drawn exclusively from their works. Greek Atticism and Roman archaism are presumably related, though the exact nature of the connection is not clear. For a cool view of this literary milieu see Champlin, *Fronto and Antonine Rome*, chs. 3-4. See now L. Holford-

Strevens, *Aulus Gellius* (Duckworth, London 1988).

11 This and other letters are used by G. W. Bowersock, in his
landmark study *Greek Sophists in the Roman Empire*
(Oxford, 1969), 71–5, to assist his diagnosis of the Antonine
era as an age of hypochondria. But can the incidence of scor-
pions be accurately correlated to that of hypochondria?

12 For the general theme see nos. 1 and 16; Champlin, *Fronto
and Antonine Rome*, ch. 8. This letter, however, has particular interest for its shrewd summary of the dialectical
method of Socrates as presented in Plato's dialogues. Protagoras, a distinguished thinker from Abdera in Thrace,
often visited Athens and was a friend of Pericles; he figures
in the dialogue which bears his name; the lesser figures
Polus and Thrasymachus were also sophistic teachers, and
appear in Plato's *Gorgias* and in book i of the *Republic*
respectively. Alcibiades, the beautiful, talented but
unscrupulous young man who was Socrates' most notorious
disciple, is memorably portrayed in the *Symposium*. In
general see W. K. C. Guthrie, *A History of Greek
Philosophy*, iii (Cambridge, 1969), also available as two
separate paperbacks, *The Sophists* and *Socrates*.

For the Cynic Diogenes see note on *Meditations*, xi. 6.

13 A particularly interesting exchange which has been much
discussed. Here Fronto is to act as prosecutor in a case
where the distinguished Athenian sophist, Herodes Atticus,
is either defendant himself or involved in some way with the
accused (perhaps even as defending counsel). Fronto seems
not to have realized how friendly Marcus himself was with
Herodes. It is obvious that Marcus is alarmed and disturbed,
but equally clear that he does not want to pull rank and
insist on Fronto either dropping the case or conducting it
feebly; nor, to do him justice, is Fronto prepared to let
Herodes off lightly. The outcome of the trial is unknown,
but Fronto and Herodes seem eventually to be on easy terms
(ii. 221 and 235 Haines, passages in which Fronto declares
that 'Herodes and I are now on the best of terms, despite

the speech being published' ('quamquam extet oratio')). Presumably this means the speech discussed in these letters; this supports the view that it was not Herodes himself who was on trial on this occasion. Other sources give us further insight into Herodes' high-handed and indeed tyrannical behaviour at Athens: see especially Philostratus, *Lives of the Sophists*, ii. 1, discussed by Bowersock, *Greek Sophists* (cited above on 11), 93–9, and by Champlin, *Fronto*, 63–4.

14 Marcus' relieved note of reassurance needs no comment, but Fronto's response is a quaint piece of self-important self-analysis with a saving note of humour. Apart from the amateur psychologizing, the letter is chiefly interesting for Fronto's criticism of Marcus' anti-social behaviour (para. 5): the indifference to parties or to the gladiatorial games fits well with the seriousness of the emperor later in life: in *Meditations*, vi. 46 he complains of the tedium of the amphitheatre (cf. also x. 8).

as the poet says: as the rest of the paragraph shows, the reference is to the epic poem of Ennius (*Annals*, book 1, fr. 2 Skutsch), who in a famous scene presented his encounter with Homer in a dream as the source of his own inspiration.

15 See n. 2 above.

16 This passage forms part of a long letter defending the value of rhetorical ornamentation and stylistic elegance against the more puritanical approach advocated originally by Plato and developed further by the Stoics (see e.g. Cicero, *On the Orator*, i. 219–33), who distrusted the extravagant use of rhetoric to blur the facts and arouse the audience's emotions. Fronto's response is that even philosophers make use of stylistic variation and different kinds of rhetorical device. It is a theme he regularly debates with Marcus: cf. nos. 6 and 12. The categorizing of poetic and rhetorical styles in the first paragraph here is an interesting and characteristic document of ancient literary criticism, which went in for epigrammatic evaluations, often inherited as stock judgements (cf. Quintilian, *On the Education of an Orator*, x. 1).

like Menelaus at the feast: an allusion to *Iliad* ii. 408, where Menelaus comes along uninvited to the sacrifice his brother is preparing before the army enters battle.

Falernian . . . Cretan or Seguntian: a delightful inversion of a moralistic commonplace, namely the praise of homegrown produce, however simple, as opposed to luxury imports. Normally the troublesome guest might be expected to demand richer fare; but here the rejected Falernian is the noblest of Italian wines, whereas the wine the rude guest wants, though imported, is certainly inferior and may be just popular plonk, obtainable from the city tavern.

17 The subject Fronto treats in this letter or miniature essay—bereavement and premature loss—ensures its lasting interest. It is striking that he goes to such lengths in questioning the gods and Providence, and rejecting the consolations of philosophy (consolations which we see Marcus applying to his own misgivings or uncertainties in the *Meditations*). The letter and its arguments may be compared with a number of other ancient works on this theme, notably Servius Sulpicius' letter of consolation to Cicero following the death of the latter's daughter Tullia (*Letters to his Friends*, iv. 5; Cicero's reply, iv. 6, also survives). See further note on *Meditations* ii. 14. Such arguments often seem cold and unhelpful to the modern reader, and Fronto's bitter outburst, although expressed with plenty of stylistic elegance, may strike a chord more readily. Less sympathetic to us is the extended statement of his own merits which concludes the letter; but Romans were less inclined to false modesty or playing down of their achievements than the tight-lipped British. We should also reflect that Fronto sees himself as very close to his own death: the review of his career implies it has reached its end, and can be compared with an epitaph in the first person: similar in its form and effect is the famous speech of Dido before she stabs herself in Virgil's *Aeneid* (iv. 657 ff.): 'My life is ended, and I have run the full course that Fortune granted me, and now a mighty shadow of me

will journey beneath the earth. I founded a glorious city, I saw my people's walls rising, I avenged my husband and exacted punishment from my treacherous brother—happy, o all too happy, if only the Trojan keels had never touched our shores!'

COMPARATIVE STYLE OF
REFERENCES TO FRONTO

This translation	Traditional title		van den Hout page (1954)	(1988)	Haines vol. and page (Loeb)
no. 1	*ad Marcum Caesarem*	iii.12	44–5	44–5	i.14–16
2	"	ii.3	26–7	27	i.128–30
3	"	ii.10	27–9	28–9	i.136–40
4	"	iii.9	43–4	43	i.50
5	"	iv.4	60–1	60–1	i.175–6
6	"	iii.1	36	35	i.52
7	"	iv.5	61–2	61–2	i.178–80
8	"	iv.6	62–3	62–3	i.180–2
9	"	v.1, 2	71	69–70	i.188
10	"	v.3, 4	71–2	70	i.188–90
11	"	v.8, 9	74–5	72–3	i.196
12	"	iii.15	47–9	47–8	i.100–2
13	"	iii.2, 3, 4	36–9	36–8	i.58–66
14	"	iv.11, 12	65–8	65–7	i.202–8
15	*ad Antoninum imp.*	ii.2	109–10	105–6	i.302–4
16	*ad Verum imp.*	i.1	131–3	133–5	ii.46–52
17	*de nepote amisso*	1, 2	220–3	235–8	ii.222–32

INDEX

The index covers the introduction and translation, but not the notes. References are to pages.

American Literature

British and Irish Literature

Children's Literature

Classics and Ancient Literature

Colonial Literature

Eastern Literature

European Literature

History

Medieval Literature

Oxford English Drama

Poetry

Philosophy

Politics

Religion

The Oxford Shakespeare

A complete list of Oxford Paperbacks, including Oxford World's Classics, Oxford Shakespeare, Oxford Drama, and Oxford Paperback Reference, is available in the UK from the Academic Division Publicity Department, Oxford University Press, Great Clarendon Street, Oxford OX2 6DP.

In the USA, complete lists are available from the Paperbacks Marketing Manager, Oxford University Press, 198 Madison Avenue, New York, NY 10016.

Oxford Paperbacks are available from all good bookshops. In case of difficulty, customers in the UK can order direct from Oxford University Press Bookshop, Freepost, 116 High Street, Oxford OX1 4BR, enclosing full payment. Please add 10 per cent of published price for postage and packing.